Current
CONTROVERSIES

Forensic Technology

P9-EMH-293

Other Books in the Current Controversies Series

Biodiversity

Blogs

Capital Punishment

Darfur

Disaster Response

Drug Trafficking

Espionage and Intelligence

Factory Farming

Global Warming

Human Trafficking

Immigration

Online Social Networking

Poverty and Homelessness

Prisons

Racism

Resistant Infections

The U.S. Economy

The World Economy

Urban Sprawl

Violence Against Women

Forensic Technology

Sylvia Engdahl, Book Editor

GREENHAVEN PRESS
A part of Gale, Cengage Learning

Detroit • New York • San Francisco • New Haven, Conn • Waterville, Maine • London

GALE
CENGAGE Learning

Christine Nasso, *Publisher*
Elizabeth Des Chenes, *Managing Editor*

© 2011 Greenhaven Press, a part of Gale, Cengage Learning

Gale and Greenhaven Press are registered trademarks used herein under license.

For more information, contact:
Greenhaven Press
27500 Drake Rd.
Farmington Hills, MI 48331-3535
Or you can visit our Internet site at gale.cengage.com

ALL RIGHTS RESERVED.
No part of this work covered by the copyright herein may be reproduced, transmitted, stored, or used in any form or by any means graphic, electronic, or mechanical, including but not limited to photocopying, recording, scanning, digitizing, taping, Web distribution, information networks, or information storage and retrieval systems, except as permitted under Section 107 or 108 of the 1976 United States Copyright Act, without the prior written permission of the publisher.

For product information and technology assistance, contact us at

Gale Customer Support, 1-800-877-4253
For permission to use material from this text or product, submit all requests online at www.cengage.com/permissions

Further permissions questions can be emailed to permissionrequest@cengage.com

Articles in Greenhaven Press anthologies are often edited for length to meet page requirements. In addition, original titles of these works are changed to clearly present the main thesis and to explicitly indicate the author's opinion. Every effort is made to ensure that Greenhaven Press accurately reflects the original intent of the authors. Every effort has been made to trace the owners of copyrighted material.

Cover image copyright © Jochen Tack/Alamy.

LIBRARY OF CONGRESS CATALOGING-IN-PUBLICATION DATA

Forensic technology / Sylvia Engdahl, book editor.
    p. cm. -- (Current controversies)
    Includes bibliographical references and index.
    ISBN 978-0-7377-4911-3 (hbk.) -- ISBN 978-0-7377-4912-0 (pbk.)
    1. Forensic sciences--Juvenile literature. 2. Forensic sciences--Technological innovations--Juvenile literature. 3. Criminal investigation--Juvenile literature. I. Engdahl, Sylvia.
    HV8073.8.F67 2010
    363.25--dc22
                                        2010013956

Printed in the United States of America
1 2 3 4 5 6 7 14 13 12 11 10

ACC LIBRARY SERVICES
AUSTIN, TX

Contents

Foreword   **13**

Introduction   **16**

Chapter 1: Is Forensic Technology Unreliable?

Chapter Preface   **21**

Yes: Many Common Forensic Technologies Have Not Been Scientifically Validated

The Quality of Forensic Investigation Varies   **24**
Widely Due to a Lack of Standards
National Research Council

With National Research Council approval and support, the National Academy of Sciences conducted an investigation of forensic technology and in 2009 issued a report stating that much of it is not based on sound science. New procedures, more education, accreditation of laboratories and practitioners, and further research were recommended.

More Research in Forensic Science Is   **35**
Needed to Prevent Wrongful Convictions
Peter Neufeld

Many innocent people have been convicted on the basis of faulty forensic evidence, which judges and juries have been misled to believe is based on science. The support of Congress in implementing the recommendations of the National Academy of Sciences' 2009 report is needed.

Both Fraud and Error in Forensic   **44**
Investigation Are Common
Radley Balko and Roger Koppl

Charlatans have often taken advantage of judges' and juries' ignorance about forensic technologies, but there have been even more instances of mistakes on the part of conscientious investigators. The system must be reformed and quality control measures must be instituted.

There Is No Scientific Basis for Trusting   50
Fingerprint Evidence
    Simon A. Cole

In recent years, there has been growing controversy over the validity and legal admissibility of fingerprint evidence. Judges believe that fingerprinting is reliable, but an increasing number of experts now agree that there is no scientific evidence for such a conclusion.

The Defense Now Has the Right to   61
Question Forensic Analysts During Trials
    Lyle Denniston

The U.S. Supreme Court has recently ruled that if a crime lab report is introduced as evidence in a trial, the defense has the right to cross-examine the person who prepared it. The Court's majority opinion cited many published reports on the unreliability of forensic evidence.

No: Forensic Evidence Is Not as Unreliable as Recent Reports Suggest

Efforts to Solve the Problems of Forensic   64
Science Are Already Underway
    Tabatha Wethal

The state of forensics is not as bad as the 2009 National Academy of Sciences report suggests, for most of the problems cited were already known to those working in the field, and many of the steps it recommends are already being taken. Poor training of analysts is caused by lack of funding.

The Official Report on the State of   71
Forensics Is Interfering with Prosecutions
    Barry Matson

The 2009 National Academy of Sciences report overlooked all that prosecutors and forensic professionals do to protect the innocent. Its attack on established investigative techniques has already had a negative impact on prosecutors who are seeking the truth.

Forensic Technology Has Been Wrongly   79
Criticized as Unscientific
    Crime Lab Report

Forensic technologies have been developed over a long period of time by qualified researchers, and there is no evidence that they are unreliable. Their critics are uninformed about the ways in which they have been validated. All scientific evidence requires human interpretation.

Chapter 2: Does the "*CSI* Effect" Influence Verdicts in Jury Trials?

Chapter Preface   89

Yes: Juries and Lawyers Are Affected by Fictional Portrayals of Crime Investigation

The TV Drama *CSI* Is Affecting How Jurors   91
React in Real-Life Trials
Richard Willing

So many people watch the television series *CSI: Crime Scene Investigation* that it is having an effect on how lawyers prepare their cases and choose juries. Many believe juror familiarity with *CSI* helps the defense, but on the other hand it may also help prosecutors.

The *CSI* Effect Is Leading to   98
Unwarranted Acquittals
Jeffrey Heinrick

Television-educated jurors are less likely to convict someone who is guilty because the techniques they have observed in fictional cases have not been used. It may eventually become standard procedure in pre-jury screening to make sure that jurors understand forensic technology.

Judges Should Take Steps to Counter   106
CSI's Influence on Jurors
Joshua K. Marquis

CSI fosters myths about how crime scene investigators work, and it also leads jurors to expect forensic evidence where in many cases it does not exist. As a result, other evidence that once would have led to a conviction is discounted. Judges should do more to combat this trend.

The Criminal Litigation Process Is Being   113
Altered by Fear of the *CSI* Effect
Tamara F. Lawson

A potential juror's exposure to the distorted view of criminal prosecution created by *CSI* sways his or her analysis of real evidence. Lawyers and judges are changing their tactics to deal with this, and it has immeasurably changed the way criminal litigation is conducted today. No matter what it is called, there is a real phenomenon that must be controlled to ensure fair trials.

No: There Is No Evidence That TV Fiction Has Changed Jury Behavior

Expectation of Forensic Evidence Has   122
No Bearing on Jurors' Decisions
Donald E. Shelton

A study of 1,000 prospective jurors found that although *CSI* viewers had higher expectations for scientific evidence than non-*CSI* viewers, these expectations had little, if any, bearing on the respondents' willingness to convict.

The *CSI* Effect Exists Only in the Minds   132
of Those Who Propose It
Kimberlianne Podlas

There is no empirical evidence that a *CSI* Effect exists; claims that it does are based merely on anecdotes about cases that law enforcement lost when it believed it should have won. The alleged effect does not warrant criminal justice reforms or increased latitude for prosecutors.

Wide Media Coverage of the *CSI* Effect   141
May Itself Influence Jury Reactions
Simon A. Cole and Rachel Dioso-Villa

It is often claimed by the media that the *CSI* Effect is an established phenomenon and that it is disadvantageous to prosecutors, although legal scholars have pointed out that it might instead work to their advantage. These claims may be either a self-fulfilling prophecy or a self-denying one.

Chapter 3: Can New Forensic Technologies Determine If Someone Is Lying?

Chapter Preface   151

Yes: New Technologies Can Detect Concealment of Information or Dishonesty

Recordings of Brain Activity Show Whether   **154**
a Fact Is Stored in Someone's Memory

Sam Simon

A new forensic technique known as Brain Fingerprinting can determine from brain activity whether a person's memory contains certain facts about a crime. It does not show guilt or innocence, but it can reveal that claims to have no knowledge of those facts are false.

Brain Scanning Accurately Detects Lies   **164**
During Experiments

Malcolm Ritter

Research is being done on using fMRI (functional magnetic resonance imaging), a common medical process, as a tool for lie detection. Developers have obtained 90 percent accuracy and hope that after further study, the technique will become admissible in court.

Hand-Held Lie Detectors May Be Useful   **172**
for Screening Purposes

Bill Dedman

A new hand-held lie detector is being used by the military in war zones, although not on U.S. personnel. It is much less complex and thus even less accurate than a polygraph, but its proponents say it serves to show which people out of a large group should be questioned further.

No: Lie Detection Technologies Are Not Accurate Enough to Use in Criminal Investigations

The Assumption That Physical Reactions   **182**
Can Detect Lying Is Not Valid

Melissa Mitchell

Brain-based technologies have been promoted as effective in detection of lies, but some scholars believe they are based on false assumptions and will not work any better than polygraphs, which have been increasingly dismissed as unreliable.

Brain Scanning Has Not Been Sufficiently   187
Tested for Public Use

Aalok Mehta

Studies of fMRI lie detection have been successful in
controlled lab settings, but it is much too soon to say it
will work in real-life situations. It is reckless and unethical to put it into use, when little is known about its limitations, and jurors tend to give too much weight to neuroscience.

Voice Stress Analysis Cannot Adequately   191
Distinguish Lies from Truth

Kelly R. Damphousse

Although voice stress analysis, which detects a person's
stress level by recording voice patterns, is used by many
law enforcement agencies, studies have found that it is
no better at detecting lies than flipping a coin. However,
knowing that it is being used does deter people from lying.

Chapter 4: What Improvements in Forensic Technology Are Being Tried?

Chapter Preface   199

Improved Techniques for Analyzing Stains   202
Provide Information About Crimes

Matt Martin

New forensic technologies, such as bloodstain pattern
analysis and skin cell examination, reveal much more
about a crime scene than older methods, and far better
tools exist for analyzing substances. But not all the techniques shown on television crime shows are available.

Micro-Stamping of Firearms Is Not an   208
Effective Means of Identifying Criminals

Wendy Wang

California has a law requiring firing pins of new semiautomatic pistols to be engraved with a micro-stamped
code, but studies have found that this technology does
not work well with all guns and ammunition, and merely
linking a cartridge to a gun does not show who fired it.

DNA Testing Is Now Being Used   211
with Non-Violent Crimes

   Dan Morse

   DNA testing, once used only in cases of murder or rape,
   is now sometimes employed to solve lesser crimes. Prosecutors say this will lead to more guilty pleas, but defense lawyers fear that it will increase the odds of false
   matches; moreover, it is creating a backlog of work in
   DNA labs.

DNA Samples Can Provide Clues to a   214
Crime Suspect's Physical Appearance

   Evan Pellegrino

   Studies show that it is possible to predict the hair, eye,
   and skin color of a suspect from DNA taken at a crime
   scene. This technique is not yet sophisticated enough to
   be used as evidence, but it may be a useful tool for crime
   investigation.

CT Scanning Has Many Advantages   217
over Conventional Autopsies

   Douglas Page

   Multidetector computed tomography (MDCT) scanning
   is fast, non-invasive, and can be used when conventional
   autopsies are not feasible. Furthermore, it can provide
   information about the cause of death that a conventional
   autopsy cannot.

Attempts Are Underway to Make Bite   224
Mark Analysis More Scientific

   Todd Richmond

   Bite mark analysis has long been criticized as unscientific
   and inaccurate, but now an attempt is being made to
   create a database of bite marks that will help to determine the rarity of specific bite mark characteristics. However, critics say that skin changes distort bite marks too
   much.

Soil Analysis Is Becoming a Powerful   227
Technique for Crime Investigation

   Louise Murray

New technologies for soil analysis can pinpoint the location from which dirt found at a crime scene or on a suspect has come. They are also extremely valuable for locating buried bodies, as it is possible to detect where the soil has been disturbed.

Research on Decomposing Bodies Provides
Important Data for Forensics   **232**
Mike Osborne

The Anthropological Research Facility at the University of Tennessee, generally referred to as the Body Farm, provides extremely important information about how bodies decompose. It is used not only to train criminologists but to analyze the bodies of specific crime victims.

Organizations to Contact   **235**

Bibliography   **241**

Index   **247**

Foreword

By definition, controversies are "discussions of questions in which opposing opinions clash" (Webster's Twentieth Century Dictionary Unabridged). Few would deny that controversies are a pervasive part of the human condition and exist on virtually every level of human enterprise. Controversies transpire between individuals and among groups, within nations and between nations. Controversies supply the grist necessary for progress by providing challenges and challengers to the status quo. They also create atmospheres where strife and warfare can flourish. A world without controversies would be a peaceful world; but it also would be, by and large, static and prosaic.

The Series' Purpose

The purpose of the Current Controversies series is to explore many of the social, political, and economic controversies dominating the national and international scenes today. Titles selected for inclusion in the series are highly focused and specific. For example, from the larger category of criminal justice, Current Controversies deals with specific topics such as police brutality, gun control, white collar crime, and others. The debates in Current Controversies also are presented in a useful, timeless fashion. Articles and book excerpts included in each title are selected if they contribute valuable, long-range ideas to the overall debate. And wherever possible, current information is enhanced with historical documents and other relevant materials. Thus, while individual titles are current in focus, every effort is made to ensure that they will not become quickly outdated. Books in the Current Controversies series will remain important resources for librarians, teachers, and students for many years.

In addition to keeping the titles focused and specific, great care is taken in the editorial format of each book in the series. Book introductions and chapter prefaces are offered to provide background material for readers. Chapters are organized around several key questions that are answered with diverse opinions representing all points on the political spectrum. Materials in each chapter include opinions in which authors clearly disagree as well as alternative opinions in which authors may agree on a broader issue but disagree on the possible solutions. In this way, the content of each volume in Current Controversies mirrors the mosaic of opinions encountered in society. Readers will quickly realize that there are many viable answers to these complex issues. By questioning each author's conclusions, students and casual readers can begin to develop the critical thinking skills so important to evaluating opinionated material.

Current Controversies is also ideal for controlled research. Each anthology in the series is composed of primary sources taken from a wide gamut of informational categories including periodicals, newspapers, books, U.S. and foreign government documents, and the publications of private and public organizations. Readers will find factual support for reports, debates, and research papers covering all areas of important issues. In addition, an annotated table of contents, an index, a book and periodical bibliography, and a list of organizations to contact are included in each book to expedite further research.

Perhaps more than ever before in history, people are confronted with diverse and contradictory information. During the Persian Gulf War, for example, the public was not only treated to minute-to-minute coverage of the war, it was also inundated with critiques of the coverage and countless analyses of the factors motivating U.S. involvement. Being able to sort through the plethora of opinions accompanying today's major issues, and to draw one's own conclusions, can be a complicated and frustrating struggle. It is the editors' hope that Current Controversies will help readers with this struggle.

Introduction

"The main cause of the underuse of forensic technology is that it is very expensive."

In recent years, public interest in forensic technology has grown, largely because of such television dramas as *CSI: Crime Scene Investigation* and others like it. However, these shows offer a somewhat distorted picture of forensics. They imply that when an investigator finds evidence, this will immediately lead to the arrest and conviction of whoever committed the crime. That is not how it works in real life. The people who investigate crime scenes are usually not the same people who do laboratory work; evidence must be sent away to a lab and it is often many weeks, even months, before a report on it is received. Moreover, some of the technologies shown on television are either so new that few police departments have access to them or they do not even exist yet.

Also, as is explained in Chapter One of this book, most existing forensic technologies have not been scientifically validated and are not nearly as foolproof as either the public or the legal profession supposes. They are not the same kind of "technology" as computer technology, which turns out products meeting uniform specifications—they involve human interpretation. This would be true even if their reliability had been measured by science.

Forensic technology is nevertheless extremely valuable in criminal investigations, whether or not it produces evidence admissible in court. But unfortunately, it is not as widely utilized as is generally assumed. In the case of DNA testing—by far the most reliable of the various technologies available—underuse prevents both the conviction of criminals who might otherwise be caught and the exoneration of innocent persons who have been wrongly convicted. According to the *National Forensic DNA Study Report* issued in 2003 by Washington State University, as of that time there were approximately 52,000 homicide cases, 169,000 rape cases, and 264,000 property crime cases with biological evidence that had not been submitted to a laboratory for analysis. In addition, over 57,000 cases had been submitted but had not yet been analyzed. Processing time in state laboratories for rape kits was averaging 23.9 weeks; in local laboratories it was even longer. One reason some police departments do not submit evidence to labs is that it takes too long to get results.

However, the main cause of the underuse of forensic technology is that it is very expensive. Most police departments do not have sufficient funds to invest in new technologies or even to make extensive use of older ones. "The biggest deterrent to using forensic technology to its fullest crime solving—or exonerating—capacity is cost," says Chris Asplen in the August 2009 issue of *Forensic Magazine*. "Increasingly, the failure to use DNA technology comes not from a lack of education nor of desire. It comes from a lack of financial resources."

Asplen goes on to argue that a recent U.S. Supreme Court decision giving the defense the right to cross-examine experts who have produced forensic evidence in a case will make this problem worse. "The most variable expense component of DNA testing is the cost of labor," he points out. "The more a prosecutor's office has to call their analysts to testify, the more expensive every test becomes. The more expensive the test, the fewer tests that can be run. . . . The more time an analyst spends in court, the less time they spend in the lab."

Although the backlog has now been reduced in some jurisdictions, crime labs still do not have enough money to expand their facilities or to hire as many technicians as are needed; and there is a shortage of trained technicians in any case. The National Institute of Justice (NIJ), which defines a backlogged case as one that has not been tested for thirty days after being submitted to a crime lab, states that there was a national backlog of 70,693 DNA cases as of January 1, 2008. At NIJ's Web site it explains, "Federal funding has made significant progress toward clearing old cases from crime laboratories. Today, backlogs are of relatively new cases, but they continue to be a problem in many laboratories because demand for DNA testing services is increasing faster than the capacity of laboratories to process cases."

A special report posted at MSNBC.com on February 23, 2010, is less optimistic about progress. "With crime labs struggling under backlogs that already reach back years in many cities and states, budget cuts driven by the recession are threatening to make credible crime scene analysis a lost art," it says, citing the opinion of law enforcement officials and forensic specialists. "Staffs and training time are shrinking as budgets are cut. Elected officials know it's political suicide to take police officers off the street, so if jobs have to go, the cuts typically come in back-office services like crime lab analysis."

And with underfunding and inadequate staffing come errors and mishandling of evidence. For example, the crime lab in Houston has been shut down twice in the last eight years because of contaminated DNA samples, mistake-filled analysis, and even fraudulent lab reports, the MSNBC report states. At least six men in that jurisdiction have been released from prison after the Innocence Project, an advocacy group for wrongly convicted prisoners, uncovered such mistakes, and at least three others may have been executed. About 160 cases are being investigated in which "serious questions have been raised about the crime lab's performance," and in a separate Houston investigation, error rates among fingerprint samples tested by auditors were as high as 81 percent.

All experts agree that a great deal of improvement in the practice of forensic science is needed. Where there is controversy, it concerns the degree of confidence that can be placed in the results produced by specific forensic technologies, and the extent to which such evidence should be relied on. Many of these technologies show great promise, but without more funding for research and adequate implementation, that promise cannot be fulfilled. In addition to the issue of reliability, *Current Controversies: Forensic Technologies* explores other important topics in the debate over forensic investigation, including the influence of television shows, such as *CSI*, on juries; the effectiveness of new lie detection technologies; and potential improvements in forensics that will enhance the reliability of the field in years to come.

Is Forensic
Technology Unreliable?

Chapter Preface

In 2005, Congress passed a law authorizing the National Academy of Sciences (NAS) to conduct a study on forensic science and to "make recommendations for maximizing the use of forensic technologies and techniques to solve crimes, investigate deaths, and protect the public." The NAS was also instructed to identify potential scientific advances in forensics, recommend ways of increasing the number of qualified forensic scientists, and disseminate guidelines to help ensure quality and consistency in the use of forensic technologies, among other things. Approved by the National Research Council, a committee was established to carry out this study, and in 2009 it published its report.

The conclusions reached by the committee were a surprise to most people—although not to forensic science professionals. The report said that except for DNA testing, forensic technologies are not based on scientific research and that giving too much weight to their results may lead to the admission of erroneous evidence in trials, sometimes even to the conviction of innocent persons. "The bottom line is simple," said the report. "In a number of forensic science disciplines, forensic science professionals have yet to establish either the validity of their approach or the accuracy of their conclusions, and the courts have been utterly ineffective in addressing this problem."

This situation has been discussed within the field for years, with many professionals recognizing the problems caused by lack of funding for research and training, as well as the need for certification of crime labs and technicians. Some of the problems were already on the way to being corrected before the report appeared. And there has been ongoing controversy among experts about the validity of specific forensic techniques. However, the public, along with judges and attorneys, has generally believed that forensic evidence is reliable. Many people were shocked to hear that its reliability is merely a matter of degree.

It is not that crime lab results are never accurate. On the contrary, they produce a great deal of valuable information. The difficulty is that there is no way of knowing how accurate they are because in the case of most, there have been no scientific studies to determine their rate of error. DNA testing is an exception, since it was developed for biological research and medical purposes before being used in forensics. Other forensic technologies were developed specifically for use in solving crimes, not by scientists but by law enforcement specialists. They were put to practical use without going through the kind of testing and evaluation that is required in science.

There is no such thing as a forensic test—or a medical test, for that matter—that is 100 percent accurate. Even DNA testing, considered the "gold standard" of forensic testing, can in principle produce occasional errors, although in that case they are so rare that the chances of their occurring in forensic situations are negligible. A recent article in the *New York Times* pointed out that while the Federal Bureau of Investigation (FBI) has estimated the odds of unrelated people sharing genetic markers to be as remote as 1 in 113 billion, a very few matches have been found in Arizona's database of 65,000 felons, arousing controversy over the use of such databases—although the way the searching was done means this could not happen under ordinary circumstances. In the case of other forensic techniques, however—even fingerprint identification—the rate of error has never been measured. It has often been assumed, especially by judges and juries, that they are not subject to error when performed by competent technicians; and many people believe this misconception leads to wrongful convictions.

There are quite a few known cases of innocent persons having been convicted on the basis of forensic evidence, only to be exonerated later by DNA tests. Does this happen more frequently than is justifiable? Should technologies unverified by science be used at all? Not doing so might protect some of the innocent, but on the other hand suspects are often cleared by such technologies. In any case, it is essential to public safety for those who are guilty to be caught and imprisoned, and most law enforcement professionals believe that evidence obtained from imperfect forensic techniques is better than nothing. It is agreed that most forensic technologies are useful aids to crime investigation. The controversy concerns which kinds of forensic evidence should be admissible in court, and how much courts should rely on it.

The Quality of Forensic Investigation Varies Widely Due to a Lack of Standards

National Research Council

The National Research Council functions under the auspices of the National Academy of Sciences, the National Academy of Engineering, and the Institute of Medicine. Collectively, these four organizations are referred to as the National Academies. In 2005, Congress authorized the National Academy of Sciences (NAS) to conduct a study of forensic science. In 2006, the NAS established a committee operating under the project title "Identifying the Needs of the Forensic Science Community." Approved by the Governing Board of the National Research Council, the project also brought together the Committee on Science, Technology, and Law Policy and Global Affairs and the Committee on Applied and Theoretical Statistics Division on Engineering and Physical Science to produce the report from which the following excerpt is taken.

For decades, the forensic science disciplines have produced valuable evidence that has contributed to the successful prosecution and conviction of criminals as well as to the exoneration of innocent people. Over the last two decades, advances in some forensic science disciplines, especially the use of DNA technology, have demonstrated that some areas of forensic science have great additional potential to help law enforcement identify criminals. Many crimes that may have gone unsolved are now being solved because forensic science is helping to identify the perpetrators.

Those advances, however, also have revealed that, in some cases, substantive information and testimony based on faulty

National Research Council, *Strengthening Forensic Science in the United States: A Path Forward*. Washington DC: National Academies Press, 2009. Copyright © 2009 by the National Academy of Sciences, courtesy of the National Academies Press, Washington, D.C. All rights reserved. Reproduced by permission.

forensic science analyses may have contributed to wrongful convictions of innocent people. This fact has demonstrated the potential danger of giving undue weight to evidence and testimony derived from imperfect testing and analysis. Moreover, imprecise or exaggerated expert testimony has sometimes contributed to the admission of erroneous or misleading evidence.

Further advances in the forensic science disciplines will serve three important purposes. First, further improvements will assist law enforcement officials in the course of their investigations to identify perpetrators with higher reliability. Second, further improvements in forensic science practices should reduce the occurrence of wrongful convictions, which reduces the risk that true offenders continue to commit crimes while innocent persons inappropriately serve time. Third, any improvements in the forensic science disciplines will undoubtedly enhance the Nation's ability to address the needs of homeland security.

Numerous professionals in the forensic science community and the medical examiner system have worked for years to achieve excellence in their fields, aiming to follow high ethical norms, develop sound professional standards, ensure accurate results in their practices, and improve the processes by which accuracy is determined. Although the work of these dedicated professionals has resulted in significant progress in the forensic science disciplines in recent decades, major challenges still face the forensic science community. It is therefore unsurprising that Congress instructed this committee to, among other things, "assess the present and future resource needs of the forensic science community," "make recommendations for maximizing the use of forensic technologies and techniques," "make recommendations for programs that will increase the number of qualified forensic scientists and medical examiners," and "disseminate best practices and guidelines concerning the collection and analysis of forensic evidence to help ensure quality and consistency in the use of forensic technologies and techniques." These are among the pressing issues facing the forensic science community. The best professionals in the forensic science disciplines invariably are hindered in their work because these and other problems persist.

The length of the congressional charge and the complexity of the material under review made the committee's assignment challenging. In undertaking it, the committee first had to gain an understanding of the various disciplines within the forensic science community, as well as the community's history, its strengths and weaknesses, and the roles of the people and agencies that constitute the community and make use of its services. In so doing, the committee was able to better comprehend some of the major problems facing the forensic science community and the medical examiner system. A brief review of some of these problems is illuminating.

Disparities in the Forensic Science Community

There are great disparities among existing forensic science operations in federal, state, and local law enforcement jurisdictions and agencies. This is true with respect to funding, access to analytical instrumentation, the availability of skilled and well-trained personnel, certification, accreditation, and oversight. As a result, it is not easy to generalize about current practices within the forensic science community. It is clear, however that any approach to overhauling the existing system needs to address and help minimize the community's current fragmentation and inconsistent practices.

Although the vast majority of criminal law enforcement is handled by state and local jurisdictions, these entities often are sorely lacking in the resources (money, staff, training, and equipment) necessary to promote and maintain strong forensic science laboratory systems. By comparison, federal programs are often much better funded and staffed. It is also noteworthy that the resources, the extent of services, and the amount of expertise that medical examiners and forensic pathologists can provide vary widely in different jurisdictions. As a result, the depth, reliability, and overall quality of substantive information arising from the forensic examination of evidence available to the legal system vary substantially across the country.

Lack of Mandatory Standardization, Certification, and Accreditation

The fragmentation problem is compounded because operational principles and procedures for many forensic science disciplines are not standardized or embraced, either between or within jurisdictions. There is no uniformity in the certification of forensic practitioners, or in the accreditation of crime laboratories. Indeed, most jurisdictions do not require forensic practitioners to be certified, and most forensic science disciplines have no mandatory certification programs. Moreover, accreditation of crime laboratories is not required in most jurisdictions. Often there are no standard protocols governing forensic practice in a given discipline. And, even when protocols are in place (e.g., SWG [Scientific Working Group] standards), they often are vague and not enforced in any meaningful way. In short, the quality of forensic practice in most disciplines varies greatly because of the absence of adequate training and continuing education, rigorous mandatory certification and accreditation programs, adherence to robust performance standards, and effective oversight. These shortcomings obviously pose a continuing and serious threat to the quality and credibility of forensic science practice.

The Broad Range of Forensic Science Disciplines

The term "forensic science" encompasses a broad range of forensic disciplines, each with its own set of technologies and practices. In other words, there is wide variability across forensic science disciplines with regard to techniques, methodologies, reliability, types and numbers of potential errors, research, general acceptability, and published material. Some of the forensic science disciplines are laboratory based (e.g., nuclear and mitochondrial DNA analysis, toxicology and drug analysis); others are based on expert interpretation of observed patterns (e.g., fingerprints, writing samples, toolmarks, bite marks, and specimens such as hair). The "forensic science community," in turn, consists of a host of practitioners, including scientists (some with advanced degrees) in the fields of chemistry, biochemistry, biology, and medicine; laboratory technicians; crime scene investigators; and law enforcement officers. There are very important differences, however, between forensic laboratory work and crime scene investigations. There are also sharp distinctions between forensic practitioners who have been trained in chemistry, biochemistry, biology, and medicine (and who bring these disciplines to bear in their work) and technicians who lend support to forensic science enterprises. . . .

With the exception of nuclear DNA analysis, . . . no forensic method has been rigorously shown to have the capacity to consistently . . . demonstrate a connection between evidence and a specific individual or source.

The committee decided early in its work that it would not be feasible to develop a detailed evaluation of each discipline in terms of its scientific underpinning, level of development, and ability to provide evidence to address the major types of questions raised in criminal prosecutions and civil litigation. However, the committee solicited testimony on a broad range of forensic science disciplines and sought to identify issues relevant across definable classes of disciplines. As a result of listening to this testimony and reviewing related written materials, the committee found substantial evidence indicating that the level of scientific development and evaluation varies substantially among the forensic science disciplines.

Problems Relating to the Interpretation of Forensic Evidence

Often in criminal prosecutions and civil litigation, forensic evidence is offered to support conclusions about "individualization" (sometimes referred to as "matching" a specimen to a particular individual or other source) or about classification of the source of the specimen into one of several categories. With the exception of nuclear DNA analysis, however, no forensic method has been rigorously shown to have the capacity to consistently, and with a high degree of certainty, demonstrate a connection between evidence and a specific individual or source. In terms of scientific basis, the analytically based disciplines generally hold a notable edge over disciplines based on expert interpretation. But there are important variations among the disciplines relying on expert interpretation. For example, there are more established protocols and available research for fingerprint analysis than for the analysis of bite marks. There also are significant variations within each discipline. For example, not all fingerprint evidence is equally good, because the true value of the evidence is determined by the quality of the latent fingerprint image. These disparities between and within the forensic science disciplines highlight a major problem in the forensic science community: The simple reality is that the interpretation of forensic evidence is not always based on scientific studies to determine its validity. This is a serious problem. Although research has been done in some disciplines, there is a notable dearth of peer-reviewed, published studies establishing the scientific bases and validity of many forensic methods.

The Need for Research to Establish Limits and Measures of Performance

In evaluating the accuracy of a forensic analysis, it is crucial to clarify the type of question the analysis is called on to address. Thus, although some techniques may be too imprecise to permit accurate identification of a specific individual, they may still provide useful and accurate information about questions of classification. For example, microscopic hair analysis may provide reliable evidence on some characteristics of the individual from which the specimen was taken, but it may not be able to reliably match the specimen with a specific individual. However, the definition of the appropriate question is only a first step in the evaluation of the performance of a forensic technique. A body of research is required to establish the limits and measures of performance and to address the impact of sources of variability and potential bias. Such research is sorely needed, but it seems to be lacking in most of the forensic disciplines that rely on subjective assessments of matching characteristics. These disciplines need to develop rigorous protocols to guide these subjective interpretations and pursue equally rigorous research and evaluation programs. The development of such research programs can benefit significantly from other areas, notably from the large body of research on the evaluation of observer performance in diagnostic medicine and from the findings of cognitive psychology on the potential for bias and error in human observers.

The Admission of Forensic Science Evidence in Litigation

Forensic science experts and evidence are used routinely in the service of the criminal justice system. DNA testing may be used to determine whether sperm found on a rape victim came from an accused party; a latent fingerprint found on a gun may be used to determine whether a defendant handled the weapon; drug analysis may be used to determine whether pills found in a person's possession were illicit; and an autopsy may be used to determine the cause and manner of death of a murder victim. In order for qualified forensic science experts to testify competently about forensic evidence, they must first find the evidence in a usable state and properly preserve it. A latent fingerprint that is badly smudged when found cannot be usefully saved, analyzed, or explained. An inadequate drug sample may be insufficient to allow for proper analysis. And, DNA tests performed on a contaminated or otherwise compromised sample cannot be used reliably to identify or eliminate an individual as the perpetrator of a crime. These are important matters involving the proper processing of forensic evidence. The law's greatest dilemma in its heavy reliance on forensic evidence, however, concerns the question of whether—and to what extent—there is *science* in any given forensic science discipline.

Two very important questions should underlie the law's admission of and reliance upon forensic evidence in criminal trials: (1) the extent to which a particular forensic discipline is founded on a reliable scientific methodology that gives it the capacity to accurately analyze evidence and report findings and (2) the extent to which practitioners in a particular forensic discipline rely on human interpretation that could be tainted by error, the threat of bias, or the absence of sound operational procedures and robust performance standards. These questions are significant. Thus, it matters a great deal whether an expert is qualified to testify about forensic evidence and whether the evidence is sufficiently reliable to merit a fact finder's reliance on the truth that it purports to support. Unfortunately, these important questions do not always produce satisfactory answers in judicial decisions pertaining to the admissibility of forensic science evidence proffered in criminal trials.

In 1993, in *Daubert v. Merrell Dow Pharmaceuticals, Inc.*, the Supreme Court ruled that, under Rule 702 of the Federal

Rules of Evidence (which covers both civil trials and criminal prosecutions in the federal courts), a "trial judge must ensure that any and all scientific testimony or evidence admitted is not only relevant, but reliable." The Court indicated that the subject of an expert's testimony should be scientific knowledge, so that "evidentiary reliability will be based upon scientific validity." The Court also emphasized that, in considering the admissibility of evidence, a trial judge should focus "solely" on the expert's "principles and methodology," and "not on the conclusions that they generate." In sum, *Daubert's* requirement that an expert's testimony pertain to "scientific knowledge" established a standard of "evidentiary reliability." . . .

Law enforcement officials and the members of society they serve need to be assured that forensic techniques are reliable.

Daubert and its progeny have engendered confusion and controversy. . . . Federal appellate courts have not with any consistency or clarity imposed standards ensuring the application of scientifically valid reasoning and reliable methodology in criminal cases involving *Daubert* questions. This is not really surprising, however. The Supreme Court itself described the *Daubert* standard as "flexible." This means that, beyond questions of relevance, *Daubert* offers appellate courts no clear substantive standard by which to review decisions by trial courts. As a result, trial judges exercise great discretion in deciding whether to admit or exclude expert testimony, and their judgments are subject only to a highly deferential "abuse of discretion" standard of review. . . .

The Difference Between Judicial and Scientific Search for Truth

Prophetically, the *Daubert* decision observed that "there are important differences between the quest for truth in the courtroom and the quest for truth in the laboratory. Scientific conclusions are subject to perpetual revision. Law, on the other hand, must resolve disputes finally and quickly." But because accused parties in criminal cases are convicted on the basis of testimony from forensic science experts, much depends upon whether the evidence offered is reliable. Furthermore, in addition to protecting innocent persons from being convicted of crimes that they did not commit, we are also seeking to protect society from persons who have committed criminal acts. Law enforcement officials and the members of society they serve need to be assured that forensic techniques are *reliable*. Therefore, we must limit the risk of having the reliability of certain forensic science methodologies judicially certified before the techniques have been properly studied and their accuracy verified by the forensic science community....

There is a tremendous need for the forensic science community to improve. Judicial review, by itself, will not cure the infirmities of the forensic science community.

The adversarial process relating to the admission and exclusion of scientific evidence is not suited to the task of finding "scientific truth." The judicial system is encumbered by, among other things, judges and lawyers who generally lack the scientific expertise necessary to comprehend and evaluate forensic evidence in an informed manner, trial judges (sitting alone) who must decide evidentiary issues without the benefit of judicial colleagues and often with little time for extensive research and reflection, and the highly deferential nature of the appellate review afforded trial courts' *Daubert* rulings. Given these realities, there is a tremendous need for the forensic science community to improve. Judicial review, by itself, will not cure the infirmities of the forensic science community. The development of scientific research, training, technology, and databases associated with DNA analysis have resulted

More Research in Forensic Science Is Needed to Prevent Wrongful Convictions

Peter Neufeld

Peter Neufeld is co-director of the Innocence Project, a national nonprofit litigation and public policy organization dedicated to exonerating wrongfully convicted people through DNA testing and to reforming the criminal justice system.

I am extremely pleased to participate in this hearing reviewing the recommendations and conclusions of the National Academies of Science's (NAS) report *Strengthening Forensic Science in the United States: A Path Forward.* I am grateful for the invitation to testify before you [the Senate Committee on the Judiciary] today to share how faulty forensic science has impacted the work of the Innocence Project and our response to the NAS report.

The Innocence Project, the law enforcement community, prosecutors, and members of this committee all share the same core beliefs—that wrongful convictions are contrary to the basic principle of criminal justice; that forensic science plays a vital role in solving crime; that many forensic disciplines are in need of further validity and reliability research; and that valid and reliable forensic analyses will strengthen prosecutions, assist law enforcement in investigations, and improve public safety by ensuring that the true perpetrators of crime are identified and punished. We are proud to have collaborated frequently with police and prosecutors to identify and prosecute the real perpetrator. The first priority of our work and our advocacy has always been enhancing the truth

Peter Neufeld, "Testimony to the Senate Committee on the Judiciary, Strengthening Forensic Science in the United States," United States Senate Committee on the Judiciary, September 9, 2009. Reproduced by permission of the author.

seeking function and reliability of criminal justice, which in turn advances the cause of public safety.

The development of DNA testing has allowed the Innocence Project to help exonerate 242 factually innocent Americans—17 of whom were on death row awaiting execution. These 242 exonerees represent how the American criminal justice system can fail the people she was designed to protect. Once exonerated, we then deconstruct the wrongful convictions looking for common causes while distinguishing "one off" situations. Our research into these wrongful convictions yielded a stunning insight: unvalidated and/or improper forensics was the second-greatest contributing factor to those miscarriages of justice. Those cases demonstrate what the members of the NAS committee unanimously recognized: that the lack of scientific underpinning in commonly used non-DNA forensic science has the significant potential to mislead the criminal justice system away from the real perpetrators of crime.

The need to be as sure as possible about the validity and reliability of non-DNA forensic evidence is essential for public safety and critical to the integrity of criminal justice.

When a crime's true perpetrator is not identified, communities are less safe: among the first 241 post-conviction DNA exonerations nationwide, the real perpetrators were identified in 105 cases. In many of those cases, the real perpetrator had gone on to commit additional violent crimes while an innocent person was in prison. These perpetrators were convicted of at least 90 serious, violent crimes—including 56 rapes and 19 murders—that they committed after innocent people were convicted for their earlier crimes. Many more were implicated in violent crimes but were never convicted because the statute of limitations on the crime had run out. Each one of these rapes, murders and other violent crimes could have been prevented if law enforcement had the tools to identify the correct suspect in the first place.

DNA Testing Can Be Used in Only 10 Percent of Cases

Although DNA is unparalleled in its ability to dispositively prove innocence or guilt, biological evidence that can be subjected to DNA testing is only available and affords proof in a minority of violent crimes. Some crime lab directors estimate that a mere 10 percent of the cases lend themselves to DNA testing; consequently, DNA testing cannot help us identify the truth in the remaining 90 percent of cases, many of which involve some form of forensic evidence. Therefore, the need to be as sure as possible about the validity and reliability of non-DNA forensic evidence is essential for public safety and critical to the integrity of criminal justice.

However, the NAS report alarmingly observes that many of the commonly used non-DNA forensic assays [testing] have not been scientifically validated, and there is no formal apparatus in place to do so for new and emerging forensic technologies. Many forensic techniques—such as hair microscopy, bite mark comparisons, latent fingerprint comparisons, firearm/tool mark analysis and shoe and tire print comparisons—have never been sufficiently validated to permit an examiner to assert that a particular defendant is the "source" of the trace or impression evidence recovered from the crime scene. Moreover, there has been almost no research to establish the limits and measures of performance and to address the sources of variability and potential for inadvertent bias, despite the fact that these types of studies are routine in other applied sciences such as medicine and engineering. Finally, even for forensic disciplines that have been properly validated, imprecise or exaggerated expert report writing and testimony can lead to the admission of erroneous or misleading testimony.

Assertions [from non-DNA forensic evidence] are accepted and repeated as fact, leaving juries with the false impression that the evidence is more scientific than it is.

In contrast, DNA typing had its start in the nation's premier academic research centers, and scientists validated its analytical methods before it was ever applied to the investigation of crime. When it was in its relative infancy, the NAS embarked on not one but two thorough reviews of empirical data to establish standards for the interpretation of casework results and set limits on what an analyst could reliably and scientifically say about the probative value of the DNA results. From research lab to clinical lab and from clinical lab to crime lab, forensic DNA testing developed under the same scrutiny given to medical devices. So when it entered the courtroom, there was already a tremendous body of basic and applied research reported in peer reviewed literature in highly respected scientific journals, amassed over a number of years, to support and validate it.

Non-DNA Forensic Technologies Were Not Developed Scientifically

In contrast to DNA, most of the assays and techniques used in law enforcement—for example, tool mark and bite mark comparisons—have no other application. They were developed for the purpose of investigation, prosecution and conviction and took on a life of their own without being subjected to the rigors of the scientific process. Simply as a matter of process, they often came on line in casework and in courts without following the fundamental principles of the scientific method described in Chapter 4 of the NAS report. Their assertions are accepted and repeated as fact, leaving juries with the false impression that the evidence is more scientific than it is. . . .

Many forensic disciplines are not buttressed by a vast body of basic and applied research; nor are their data presented in the premier peer review publications. For many of the pattern, trace and impression evidence forensic disciplines, there was no funding for basic academic research or even a research agenda created by an entity free of the appearance of conflict of interest to test for validity and reliability.

For the vast majority of forensic assays and techniques, there never was a conflict-free competitive grant program funding basic and applied research, nor an independent assessment of validity or reliability, nor enforceable standards in place to insure the integrity of the result in a laboratory setting. No entity comparable to the FDA [Food and Drug Administration] ever scrutinized the forensic devices and assays, nor were crime laboratories subject to mandatory accreditation and forensic service practitioners subject to certification. Enforceable parameters for interpretation of data, report writing, and courtroom testimony have also never been developed. Yet as I speak, and despite the findings of the NAS report, these assays and technologies are being used in investigations, prosecutions and convictions daily in this country despite their potential to mislead police, prosecutors, judges and juries away from the real perpetrators of crime.

The courts have not functioned well as gatekeepers of questionable scientific evidence.

Inadequate science leaves evidence open to attack and may mean that police, prosecutors, judges and juries across the country are at risk of being mislead away from the real perpetrators of crime. It erroneously steers the course of investigations, thus needlessly pursuing false leads and wasting precious resources and creating the need to reopen and renew investigations and litigate post-conviction appeals. That leads to countless manpower hours lost and significant, needless resource costs to law enforcement.

Courts Cannot Determine the Validity of Forensic Evidence

Conventional wisdom once stated that a sound defense and cross-examination would enable courts to properly assess the strength of forensic evidence. However, the NAS report unequivocally states, and the post-conviction DNA exoneration cases clearly demonstrate, that at least in criminal cases, the courts have not functioned well as gatekeepers of questionable scientific evidence, and given the lack of scientific knowledge among judges and legal practitioners, "judicial review, by itself, will not cure the infirmities of the forensic science community." Moreover, we cannot expect the courts to sort through or overcome the patchwork of standards, or to assess for themselves the reliability of a device or technique, no matter how widely used. Because of the fragmentation of the criminal justice system and in particular the fragmentation of the forensic science community, given the lack of a sound scientific foundation for many forensic technologies and assays, 50 states may be operating under 50 definitions of "science"— and therefore 50 standards of justice.

It is essential that the validity of forensic techniques be established upstream of the court, before any particular piece of evidence is considered in the adjudicative process. There is simply no substitute for requiring the application of the scientific method to each forensic assay or technology, as well as parameters for report writing and proper testimony, as part of the formal system of vetting the scientific evidence we allow in the courtroom. Indeed, for our justice system to work properly, standards must be developed and quality must be assured before the evidence is presented to the courts. . . .

The NAS notes that, despite these ongoing problems, neither the FBI [Federal Bureau of Investigation] nor the National Institute of Justice (NIJ) have, over the years, "recognized, let alone articulated, a need for change or a vision for achieving it." Although the FBI and NIJ were aware of the lack of evidence-based validation for several forensic disciplines going back many years, through both Democratic and Republican administrations, no corrective action was taken. For over 40 years, the FBI used composite bullet lead analysis in its investigations; it was only after the NAS released a report that found bullet lead analysis to be "unreliable and potentially misleading" that it was retired in the summer of 2005. Much of the research sponsored by the NIJ over the years in non-DNA forensic disciplines assumed validity. . . .

If the pharmaceutical companies took the [reins] of the research or product certification process, there is no doubt that the drugs or devices will become approved and put online for distribution more quickly. However, healthy inquiry would give rise to questions as to how comprehensively the products were reviewed given the benefit the reviewers would receive from their passage. For the same reasons we do not allow automobile makers to set vehicle performance standards. There is no justification for the nation accepting a lesser standard of oversight and conflict free independence for criminal justice than for the public's health.

Lack of Standards for Forensic Evidence Has Serious Consequences

It is critical that we all understand the real world consequences of the forensic problems. These were not incidents reflective of one bad actor, or one wayward jurisdiction; our review of the nation's DNA exonerations showed that 72 forensic analysts from 52 different labs, across 25 states had provided testimony that was inappropriate and/or significantly exaggerated the probative value of the evidence before the fact finder in either reports or live courtroom testimony. According to the NAS report, the shortcomings in education, training, certification, accreditation, and standards for testing and testifying that contributed to wrongful convictions in those cases threaten the integrity of forensic results across virtually all non-DNA forensics.

The NAS cited Brandon Mayfield's case as one that should "surely signal caution against simple, and unverified, assumptions about the reliability of fingerprint evidence." Brandon Mayfield was arrested as a material witness in the Madrid Bombings of March 2004. Several FBI fingerprint experts "matched" his print to fingerprints lifted from a plastic bag containing explosive material found at the crime scene and swore in affidavits that they were "100% certain" that the prints belonged to Mayfield. When the Spanish police ultimately arrested the real source of the fingerprint, the FBI initially defended their "mistake" as the result of poor digital image. Obviously, the two FBI experts could not have been 100% certain if the image was poor. Several major investigations followed, including one conducted by the Inspector General of the Department of Justice that found that mistakes were made, in part, because the FBI which does not require a predetermined minimum number of characteristics to draw a conclusion.

Roy Brown was convicted of a 1991 murder and spent 15 years in prison for a crime he did not commit. His conviction was secured in large part by unvalidated and improper forensic bitemark analysis, which has been shown to have "a disturbingly high false-positive error rate." Despite the fact that a leading forensic odontologist examined the bitemarks before trial and excluded Roy, the prosecution moved forward with testimony from a local dentist who stated that the seven bitemarks found on the victim's body were "entirely consistent" with Roy. Although that mark had two more upper teeth than he had, Roy was sentenced to 25 years to life.

While in prison, Roy suffered from liver disease and was in need of a liver transplant for which he was not eligible as an inmate. . . . Roy's freedom did not come until 2007, when DNA testing conclusively proved that Barry Bench committed the crime. A few days after his release, Roy received a liver transplant and lives today as a witness to how unvalidated and unreliable forensic evidence can not only take a person's freedom, but nearly his life.

Unlike Mayfield and Brown, reform will come too late for Cameron Todd Willingham. Willingham was convicted of intentionally setting fire to his house in which he and his three young daughters resided. The three girls perished in the fire. Since there was no real motive attributed to Willingham, the most significant issue in the case was whether the post-fire observations of the debris supported a finding of arson as opposed to accident. Willingham was convicted in 1993 of capital murder and sentenced to death on the strength of expert testimony provided by the state's arson investigator. He was executed by the State of Texas in 2004. The arson investigator's conclusions were based on "generally accepted," albeit an unscientific, understanding of accelerants. In the last five years, those conclusions were proven to be without scientific basis by the top arson investigators in the nation, all of whom concluded that the fire was accidental in origin. Based on evidence unearthed and published last week [September 2009], the state of Texas most likely executed an innocent man. With your support, we will minimize the possibility that tragedies like Cameron Todd Willingham, Brandon Mayfield and Roy Brown and those endured by the nation's other 241—and counting—exonerees and their families will be needlessly repeated, and we will significantly enhance the quality of justice in the United States.

Both Fraud and Error in Forensic Investigation Are Common

Radley Balko and Roger Koppl

Radley Balko is a senior editor for Reason *magazine. Roger Koppl is director of the Institute for Forensic Science Administration at Fairleigh Dickinson University.*

Last week [August 2008] the state of Mississippi terminated its 20-year relationship with medical examiner Dr. Steven Hayne. Hayne has come under fire from fellow medical examiners, criminal justice groups like the Innocence Project, and one of the authors of this [viewpoint] for his impossible workload, sloppy procedures, and questionable court testimony. In the early 1990s, Hayne and his frequent collaborator, now-disgraced forensic odontologist Dr. Michael West, helped secure murder convictions for Kennedy Brewer and Levon Brooks, both later proven innocent through DNA testing. The two were released from prison earlier this year.

Mississippi is hardly alone when it comes to bad forensic science. It now appears that Washington, D.C., may have to retry Angela O'Brien for the 2000 killing of her 2-year-old goddaughter, Brianna Blackmond, after revelations that the prosecution's star forensic witness, a physicist named Saami Shaibani, lied about his credentials in a Wisconsin murder case. These are only the most recent and dramatic examples of forensics fraud to make the headlines. Over the years, there have been plenty of other hucksters and charlatans happy to take advantage of the ignorance of juries, prosecutors, judges, and defense attorneys in very complicated and difficult-to-understand disciplines.

Radley Balko and Roger Koppl, "C.S. Oy: Forensic Science Is Badly in Need of Reform," *Slate*, August 12, 2008. Copyright © 2008 Washingtonpost/Newsweek Interactive. All rights reserved. Reproduced by permission.

But the charlatans are only half the story. Courts have also missed plenty of mistakes from well-intentioned, conscientious scientists, too. In fact, these may be even more common—and harder to catch. Studies show that crime lab fiber, paint, and body fluid analyses, for example, may consistently have error rates of 10 percent or higher. The error rate in fingerprint analysis is possibly between 1 percent and 4 percent. And bite mark evidence is notoriously unreliable though still widely used. The *Chicago Tribune* reported in July [2008] that L. Thomas Johnson—one of forensic odontology's pioneers—has been attempting to use statistical models to shore up the reliability of this discredited field. But Johnson's efforts have been hampered by new DNA testing in a 1984 murder, which concluded that the man convicted of the crime was not the source of saliva found on the victim's sweater. Johnson testified for the prosecution in that case.

Experts Are Affected by Bias

The use of forensic science in criminal trials is critically important. But reforms of the system are also desperately needed. It's not enough to weed out the incompetent scientists. We need to begin to monitor even the good ones. One major barrier to improving forensic evidence in criminal trials is that in most jurisdictions, the state has a monopoly on experts. Crime lab analysts and medical examiners (and to a lesser extent DNA technicians) typically work for the government and are generally seen as part of the prosecution's "team," much like the police and investigators. Yes, science is science, and it would be nice to believe that scientists will always get at the truth no matter whom they report to. But studies have consistently shown that even conscientious scientists can be affected by cognitive bias.

A scientist whose job performance is evaluated by a senior official in the district attorney or state attorney general's office may feel subtle pressure to return results that produce convictions. In cases in which district attorneys' offices contract work out to private labs, the labs may feel pressure—even if it's not explicit (though sometimes it is)—to produce favorable results in order to continue the relationship.

Cognitive bias can be even subtler. For some experts, merely knowing the details of a crime or discussing it with police or prosecutors beforehand can introduce significant bias to a lab technician's analysis.

A research team led by Seton Hall law professor Michael Risinger published a study in the January 2002 *California Law Review* identifying five stages of scientific analysis in which bias can affect even the most professional expert's opinion. The study was careful to note that these biases were unintentional and not the result of outright fraud. But according to the study, cognitive bias can factor into the ways in which a scientist observes the initial data, records that data, and makes calculations and also how he remembers and reinterprets his notes when preparing for trial—a problem that looms larger as time elapses between the lab work and trial testimony.

Crime labs, DNA labs, and medical examiners shouldn't serve under the same bureaucracy as district attorneys and police agencies.

Most jurors aren't aware of any of these biases; in fact, most give enormous weight to expert witnesses. Even out-and-out frauds like West and Shaibani can persuade jurors if they're presented in court as reputable experts, appear likeable, and can testify with conviction. A study of the first 86 DNA exonerations garnered by the Innocence Project estimated that faulty forensic science played a role in more than 50 percent of the wrongful convictions. While it's obviously not possible to completely eradicate bias and scientific error from the courtroom, a few simple and relatively inexpensive reforms could go a long way toward reducing it. Here are a few more recommendations:

Many Reforms Are Needed

Forensic counsel for the indigent. In many jurisdictions, indigent defendants aren't given access to their own forensic experts. As a result, the only expert witnesses are often testifying for the prosecution—experts that come prepackaged with the inherent biases noted above. This undermines the whole adversarial basis of our criminal justice system. Indigent defendants should be given vouchers to hire their own experts, who can review the forensic analysis and conclusions of each prosecution expert.

Expert independence. Crime labs, DNA labs, and medical examiners shouldn't serve under the same bureaucracy as district attorneys and police agencies. If these experts must work for the government, they should report to an independent state agency, if not the courts themselves. There should be a wall of separation between analysis and interpretation. Thus, an independent medical examiner would, for instance, perform and videotape the actual procedure in an autopsy. The prosecution and defense would then each bring in their own experts to interpret the results in court. When the same expert performs both the analysis and interpretation, defense experts are often at a disadvantage, having to rely on the notes and photos of the same expert whose testimony they're disputing.

Rivalrous redundancy. Whether the state uses its own labs or contracts out to private labs, evidence should periodically and systematically be sent out to yet another competing lab for verification. The state's labs should be made aware that their work will occasionally be checked but not told when. In addition to helping discover errors that might otherwise go undetected, the introduction of competition to government labs would all but remove any subconscious incentive to appease police and prosecutors and would strengthen the incentive for a more objective analysis.

Statistical analysis. The results from forensic labs should be regularly analyzed for statistical anomalies. Labs producing unusually high match rates should throw up red flags for further examination. For example, in 2004 Houston medical examiner Patricia Moore was found to have diagnosed shaken-baby syndrome in infant autopsies at a rate several times higher than the national average. This led to an investigation—and the reopening of several convictions that had relied on Moore's testimony.

As forensic evidence becomes more and more important in securing convictions, the need for monitoring and oversight grows exponentially.

Mask the evidence. A 2006 U.K. [United Kingdom] study by researchers at the University of Southampton found that the error rate of fingerprint analysts doubled when they were first told the circumstances of the case they were working on. Crime lab technicians and medical examiners should never be permitted to consult with police or prosecutors before performing their analysis. A dramatic child murder case, for example, may induce a greater subconscious bias to find a match than a burglary case. To the extent that it's possible, evidence should be stripped of all context before being sent to the lab. Ideally, state or city officials might hire a neutral "evidence shepherd," whose job would be to deliver crime-scene evidence to the labs and oversee the process of periodically sending evidence to secondary labs for verification.

These proposed reforms would go a long way toward correcting the problems of bias and improper incentives in the forensics system. They're also relatively inexpensive—particularly when compared with the cost of a wrongful conviction. (In the Brooks and Brewer exonerations noted above, the state of Mississippi paid for both the prosecution and defense in two high-profile murder trials, three decades of unnecessary incarceration, several rounds of appeals, and will likely have to pay each man millions of dollars in compensation.)

The continuing stories of forensics error and wrongful convictions are troubling but not all that surprising. Our criminal justice system is centuries old. It just hasn't adapted well to the dramatic advances in science and technology over the past 30 years. But as forensic evidence becomes more and more important in securing convictions, the need for monitoring and oversight grows exponentially. Every other scientific field properly requires peer review, statistical analysis, and redundancy to ensure quality and accuracy. It's past time we applied the same quality-control measures to criminal forensics, particularly given the fundamental nature of what's at stake.

There Is No Scientific Basis for Trusting Fingerprint Evidence

Simon A. Cole

Simon A. Cole is an associate professor of Criminology, Law, and Society at the University of California, Irvine. He is the author of Suspect Identities: A History of Fingerprinting and Criminal Identification.

A group of self-professed experts claims to have developed a new technique that is able to analyze objects found at a crime scene and determine whether a particular individual touched that object. The technique is so powerful that it can determine that a touch was made by a particular individual uniquely—to the exclusion of all other individuals in the world.

When this new technique is offered into evidence in a criminal trial, the defendant objects and demands scientific proof that this technique can, in fact, do what it claims to be able to do. A hearing is held to evaluate the validity of the experts' claims.

At the hearing, the experts note that training in their technique is accomplished through an apprentice system. A background in science is desirable but not necessary to practice the technique. The experts have conducted no validation studies measuring the accuracy of their determinations of identity. They have conducted no studies of the rarity of the attributes they analyze in the human population. The experts can articulate no standard that governs when a determination is made that an individual touched an object; the experts simply "know

Simon A. Cole, "The Fingerprint Controversy," *Skeptical Inquirer*, vol. 31, July–August 2007. Copyright © 2007 Committee for the Scientific Investigation of Claims of the Paranormal. Reproduced by permission.

it when they see it." Asked the error rate of their technique, the experts reply that it is zero. "A person either touched the object or he did not." When instances of error are pointed out, they claim that, in those cases, the method was "applied improperly."

Such "experts" would probably be laughed out of court. The courts would tell them to come back when they had some scientific data to show. Unless, of course, they were fingerprint experts.

It is becoming increasingly difficult to find a credentialed scientist who will argue that latent-print identification has been validated.

Over the past eight years, a battle has been waged in courtrooms, on the Internet, and in journal articles over the scientific validity and legal admissibility of fingerprint evidence. As the controversy developed, the views of the legal and scientific communities have become increasingly out of sync, with judges unanimously decreeing fingerprinting "reliable" while an increasing number of voices from the scientific community have agreed that there is no empirical basis for such a conclusion.

The debate initially took place in obscurity, in the pages of law journals and isolated courtrooms. Gradually, however, the debate has percolated into the scientific and mainstream media, fueled in part by two recent high-profile misattributions, one by the vaunted FBI [Federal Bureau of Investigation] Latent Print Unit and one that resulted in the dismantling of the Boston Police Department's latent-print unit. The National Academies are taking an interest; the controversy was the subject of a panel at a recent NAS [National Academy of Sciences] Sackler Colloquium. The editor of *Science* wrote an editorial about it. Today, we find ourselves in a peculiar situation in which the scientific and legal communities are increasingly at odds over this issue. It is becoming increasingly difficult to find a credentialed scientist who will argue that latent-print identification has been validated, while the number of scientists who agree that it has not been validated has grown. But, at the same time, not a single court has restricted the admissibility of latent-print identification, despite legal standards that clearly require proof of reliability for expert evidence to be admissible.

There is, of course, one crucial difference between the technique I imagined above and the venerated forensic technique of fingerprint (or, more precisely, "latent-print") identification: fingerprinting is not new. Unable to point to any validation studies or error measurements, longstanding use has emerged as fingerprinting's last-gasp defense. Echoing the arguments of the Ptolemains, defenders of fingerprinting have argued that techniques that have been used in criminal proceedings for a century must be accurate.

To be sure, the wide use of fingerprint identification for nearly a century counts for something. If the technique were highly inaccurate, if its accuracy was little better than chance, we would probably know it. A finding that a suspect's "friction-ridge detail" is consistent with an impression found at the scene of a crime has definite probative value in a courtroom and law-enforcement value for solving crimes and apprehending offenders. But inferring that it isn't wildly inaccurate is not the same as knowing that it is highly accurate. And it is certainly a far cry from the claims of infallibility advanced on behalf of fingerprinting.

Can science and law be reconciled? What is the empirical basis for latent-print examiners' extraordinary claims? Is fingerprinting accurate, or is it "junk science"?

Junk Science?

The lay public often interprets the term junk science to refer to claims that are just plain false. This is not exactly what Peter Huber meant when he popularized the term in his book *Galileo's Revenge*. In Huber's view, clinical ecology is not junk science because it is wrong. The clinical ecologists may eventually turn out to be right that something in the environment causes certain illnesses, but this would not alter Huber's classification of clinical ecology as junk science. Clinical ecology is junk science because it has prematurely made causal claims without sufficient proof.

It is in the latter sense that we might appropriately call latent-print identification junk science. Latent-print identification is not junk science because it is necessarily wildly inaccurate, or because it is necessarily responsible for convicting enormous numbers of people (though it is responsible for wrongly convicting some people who are known to be innocent and, no doubt, some who are not). No one has advanced any proof that latent-print identification is highly inaccurate.

It is the arguments mounted in defense of latent-print identification, not latent-print identification itself, that constitute the true junk science.

In a very rough estimate based on poor (but the only available) data, scholars have estimated that the false-positive error rate might be between 0.5 percent and 1 percent. That isn't a bad error rate (although, given that latent-print identification is deployed more than 200,000 times per year in the United States alone, it would account for a substantial number of wrongful convictions). The problem with latent-print identification is not that there is any proof that it is highly inaccurate; the problem with latent-print identification is that there isn't any measurement of how accurate it is. And, in the absence of accuracy, data defenders of fingerprinting have resorted to the worst rhetorical tricks of the pseudosciences. Latent-print evidence was admitted into courts in the early twentieth century before courts were sophisticated enough to demand accuracy data before admitting a technique that claimed the ability to make accurate source attributions. Latent-print examiners assured courts the technique was infallible, and the courts accepted the assurance. Eventually, the courts' own restatements of the supposed infallibility of fingerprinting became the evidence for that infallibility. If you ask a prosecutor for literature supporting the claim that fingerprinting has been validated, he or she is likely to refer you to a legal opinion. No one could have been more surprised than the latent-print examiners when defense attorneys announced, in the late 1990s, that the U.S. Supreme Court's opinion in the landmark 1993 expert-evidence case *Daubert v. Merrell Dow Pharmaceuticals* now required evidence of reliability—even of techniques that had been admissible for nearly a century. Cornered without any validation studies and little idea how to conduct them, the latent-print examiners and prosecutors who were charged with defending a technique that they just knew was highly accurate lapsed into drawing on all the typical rhetorical techniques used by pseudosciences. It is the arguments mounted in defense of latent-print identification, not latent-print identification itself, that constitute the true junk science. Paradoxically, defenders of fingerprinting may well have invoked pseudoscientific argument in defense of a highly accurate technique.

The Pseudoscientific Defense of Fingerprinting

Perhaps the earliest argument mounted in defense of fingerprinting was "the fingerprint examiner's fallacy". Fingerprint proponents reasoned that if all human fingerprint patterns are unique (itself no more than an assumption, though a plausible one), fingerprint identification must be 100 percent accurate. The fallacy is seductive: although it might be argued that at least one thinker recognized the fallacy early on, it took nearly a century before even sophisticated minds were able to shake free of it. Nonetheless, once considered carefully, the flaw in reasoning is obvious. One cannot infer the reliability of a source-attribution technique solely from the rarity of the target object.

The fingerprint examiner's fallacy remains the largest obstacle to clear discussion and reasoned debate over the merits of latent-print identification. Practitioners, courts, scholars, and journalists continue to state that the controversy over latent-print identification concerns whether or not all human fingerprint patterns are unique. It does not. The controversy concerns the accuracy of latent-print examiners' source attributions. Rhetorically, the fingerprint-examiner's fallacy serves defenders of fingerprinting well; it allows them to portray those "critics" who venture the now undisputed point that the accuracy of forensic fingerprint identification remains unmeasured as radical skeptics who hold to the absurd position that human beings are walking around with exact-duplicate fingerprint patterns on their fingers. It also allows latent-print examiners to purport to "prove" the uniqueness of human fingerprint formations, in the guise of addressing the accuracy of fingerprinting. If you ask a latent-print examiner for scientific proof that fingerprinting is accurate, he or she is likely to refer you to an embryology text detailing the formation of the friction-ridge skin that produces what we know as fingerprint patterns.

However, even with the fingerprint-examiner's fallacy set aside, defenders of fingerprinting have adopted rhetorical tactics that will be disturbingly familiar to scientific skeptics. Chief among them is the last refuge of the pseudoscientist: the Ptolemaic appeal to longstanding belief, a sure sign of bogus science. A leading FBI examiner told *60 Minutes*, "We have one hundred years of experience; let's make sure that that's clearly out there. And if it wasn't reliable, this certainly would have been discovered many, many years ago." The Fourth Circuit Court of Appeals noted approvingly that fingerprinting had "withstood the test of time" (*United States v. Crisp*). Some expressions of this view are almost medieval. One government brief on the issue called demanding empirical proof of the accuracy of an expert group with "one hundred years of experience" an argument "only an academic could make with a straight face" (*State v. Columbus*).

On other occasions, practitioners have argued that criminal trials in which fingerprint evidence was used constitute the scientific experiments that skeptics have demanded. Thus, in the first legal challenge to latent-print identification, the government contended that "the experts' conclusions have been tested empirically over a period of one hundred years" (*United States v. Mitchell*). The empirical testing referred to was apparently criminal cases in which a latent-print examiner said that a defendant made a certain latent print. If this assertion was not refuted somehow (by what?), the empirical tests purportedly supported the accuracy of the examiner's conclusion. This definition of a scientific experiment would, of course, be quite well suited to validate trial by ordeal; the "experiments" measure whether the technique is persuasive, not whether it is accurate. But the argument has been taken surprisingly seriously by the courts, one of which confidently opined "the methods of latent print identification can be and have been tested. They have been tested for roughly one hundred years. They have been tested in adversarial proceedings with the highest possible stakes—liberty and sometimes life" (*United States v. Havvard*). The U.S. Court of Appeal for the Third Circuit called this "implicit testing" (*United States v. Mitchell*), and the term was not meant as a criticism.

Perhaps the most astonishing claim has been that the error rate of latent-print identification is zero, even in the case of known cases of error. Latent-print examiners explain that the technique cannot err, "if the methodology . . . is properly applied".

The Accuracy of Latent-Print Identification

It is crucial to be clear about the claim that latent-print examiners are advancing. Given a "latent print" of "sufficient" quality found at a crime scene, latent-print examiners claim to be able to identify the anatomical source of that print by means of comparisons to "exemplar" prints made deliberately from candidate sources. They claim that they can exclude all other possible sources in the universe as potential sources of the latent print. Current latent-print practice guidelines brook no probabilities to be associated with these determinations; the determinations are purportedly "absolute" or "positive".

A skeptic faced with such a claim would demand proof—controlled studies in which (unlike in, say, criminal trials) the ground truth is known—that measure the rate at which examiners make correct source attributions. It is this type of study that defenders of fingerprinting have not been able to produce. The closest thing to such a study is a set of proficiency tests of unknown difficulty that have been conducted anonymously by mail since 1983. In the absence of better data, scholars have compiled the results of these studies, but latent-print examiners themselves have objected strenuously to inferring accuracy rates from this data. If we grant this argument, we are back where we started: there is no accuracy data.

Anyone unfortunate enough to be implicated in a crime by erroneous latent-print evidence would need powerful evidence to trump the fingerprint.

The very first study containing accuracy data was finally published just recently, finding very high accuracy rates in a class of trainees on latent prints of unknown difficulty; but the study contains some methodological flaws. Moreover, the authors again argue strongly against inferring accuracy rates from their own data.

In the absence of accuracy data, what then may be said about the accuracy of latent-print identification? Recently, some of the more scientifically minded examiners, unwilling to make the flawed argument that criminal trials constitute scientific trials of the ultimate accuracy of the evidence presented in them, have fallen back on the "longstanding-use" argument. Latent-print identification has been widely used in criminal-justice proceedings for nearly a century. No one knows how many deployments of latent-print analysis have been conducted during that period, but the number is clearly large. (The Bureau of Justice Statistics reports more than 200,000 requests for latent-print analysis in the U.S. alone during the year 2002.) At the same time, the number of those deployments that are known to be erroneous is quite small.

It is important to emphasize that the likelihood that misattributions would be exposed appears to be quite small. Latent-print evidence enjoys an enormously high degree of trust in our criminal-justice system, and anyone unfortunate enough to be implicated in a crime by erroneous latent-print evidence would need powerful evidence to trump the fingerprint. We must, therefore, be extremely cautious about inferring the number of actual misattributions from the number of exposed misattributions. Nonetheless, with that caveat notwithstanding, it seems obvious that if latent-print identification were highly inaccurate even the number of exposed misattributions would be higher than it is.

The courts' willingness to do violence to logic and scientific reasoning in order to avoid an uncomfortable outcome should be disturbing to all defenders of science.

It is, therefore, perhaps reasonable to conclude the century of use of latent-print identification in the criminal justice system provides evidence that the technique is not wildly inaccurate. But it is difficult to conclude much more than that.

Would this conclusion of a reasonable degree of accuracy be sufficient to meet the legal requirement of evidence of "reliability"? Probably. But, then, we return to the stubborn fact that latent-print examiners claim accuracy rates much higher than they can support. Indeed, some leaders in the field coach their peers to tell juries that the error rate is zero. And recall that identifications have to be nonprobabilistic, absolute, and claiming to exclude all potential donors in the universe.

The Abuse of Science in the Legal System

The real scandal of the fingerprint controversy is less about the ultimate accuracy of fingerprinting itself than about the abuse of science in the legal system. Judges, no doubt, have an instinctual sense that latent-print identification is highly accurate, a sense that is surely shared by many and that may not be wrong, and they probably feel that justice would not be served by restricting it. Such pragmatic decisions are not necessarily improper for judges, but they ought not be couched as "following the law" when the law clearly demands evidence of reliability. The courts' willingness to do violence to logic and scientific reasoning in order to avoid an uncomfortable outcome should be disturbing to all defenders of science, regardless of their opinion of fingerprinting. So far, the fingerprint controversy has seen enshrined in the legal record such notions as "adversarial" and "implicit" testing, "the test of time," and the "zero error rate." Perhaps the most egregious example of violence to basic scientific concepts was the court that ruled that an unpublished FBI study met the legal "peer review and publication" requirement because it had been severely criticized in journal articles that were themselves peer-reviewed and published. Another recent opinion dismissed the argument that the views of mainstream scientists were relevant to the question of whether latent-print identification had been validated. Instead, it ruled that latent-print examiners themselves could constitute the "relevant scientific com-

The Defense Now Has the Right to Question Forensic Analysts During Trials

Lyle Denniston

Lyle Denniston is a journalist who has covered the U.S. Supreme Court for nearly fifty years. He currently writes for SCOTUSblog, an Internet-based clearing house of information about the Court's work.

Expressing a heavy dose of skepticism that crime lab reports are so reliable as to be beyond question, the Supreme Court on Thursday [June 25, 2009] cleared the way for chemists and other scientists who prepare such reports to be summoned to the witness stand in criminal trials to defend their analyses. The 5-4 ruling in *Melendez-Diaz v. Massachusetts* resulted from some unusual alliances among the Justices, and continued the deep division within the Court over how to interpret the Constitution's guarantee that an individual on trial for a crime has a right to face and challenge the witnesses for the prosecution.

Justice Antonin Scalia, the Confrontation Clause's most devoted defender on the Court, wrote for the majority: "There is little reason to believe that confrontation will be useless in testing analysts' honesty, proficiency, and methodology—the features that are commonly the focus in the cross-examination of experts."

The ruling will provide for an added layer of challenge by defense lawyers to such criminal evidence as illegal drugs, fingerprints, blood spatter patterns and blood chemistry, guns and bullets, and other forms of physical evidence subjected to lab analyses, at least when the resulting reports are prepared for use as evidence in criminal trials.

Lyle Denniston, "Analysis: Law Need Not Bow to Chemistry," ScotusBlog.com, June 25, 2009. Reproduced by permission of the author.

Now, if prosecutors want to offer a crime lab report as evidence, and the report was prepared with the aim that it would be used at trial, the prosecution has to bring along the author or scientist and make them available for questioining by the defense—if the defense insists on the right to confront the analyst. It is not up to defense lawyers to summon them to the stand, but they must assert the right to confront the analyst, the Court indicated.

The [Supreme Court's] opinion recited a good deal of information from published reports about how defective crime labs and their results are.

Forensic Evidence Is Open to Challenge

The opinion recited a good deal of information from published reports about how defective crime labs and their results are, and said that claims that lab reports are the product of "neutral scientific testing" are open to challenge because such reports are not "as neutral or as reliable" as advertised. "Forensic evidence," Scalia wrote, "is not uniquely immune from the risk of manipulation."

He cited one report, for example, that said "there is wide variability across forensic science disciplines with regard to techniques, methodologies, reliability, types and numbers of potential errors, research, general acceptability, and published material."

Putting the chemist or lab technician on the stand to be tested by cross-examination, the majority said, will help "weed out not only the fraudulent analyst, but the incompetent one as well."

Still, Scalia said, the decision to compel the reports' expert authors to testify is based ultimately on the right of confrontation, not the quality of the reports or the credibility of the chemist. "We would reach the same conclusion," he wrote in a footnote, "if all analysts possessed the scientific acumen of [Nobel prize-winning chemist and physicist] Mme. [Marie] Curie and the veracity of [Catholic missionary] Mother Teresa."

To the complaints of prosecutors (and the dissenting Justices) that the decision is going to lay a heavy new burden on the preparation and analysis of criminal evidence, Justice Scalia opined that "the sky will not fall."

The best evidence of that, he wrote, is that the sky had not fallen even without the new ruling, because "many states have already adopted the constitutional rule that we announce today, while many others permit the defendant to assert (or forfeit by silence) his Confrontation Right after receiving notice of the prosecution's intent to use a forensic analyst's report. . . . There is no evidence that the criminal justice system has ground to a halt. . . . "

Moreover, Scalia said, defense lawyers may often opt not to insist on confronting a crime lab analyst, because they may conclude for strategic reasons that this might highlight rather than cast doubt on the report's results as evidence.

Scalia's opinion was supported by three of the Court's more liberal members—Justices Ruth Bader Ginsburg, David H. Souter and John Paul Stevens—and by another conservative like Scalia: Justice Clarence Thomas. Thomas filed a separate concurrence, putting some limits on what he understood the sweep of the ruling might be.

Justice Anthony M. Kennedy, joined by two conservatives, Chief Justice John G. Roberts, Jr., and Justice Samuel A. Alito, Jr., and a member of the liberal bloc, Justice Stephen G. Breyer. Kennedy began his dissent with a sweeping challenge: "The Court sweeps away an accepted rule governing the admission of scientific evidence. Until today, scientific evidence could be introduced into evidence without testimony from the 'analyst' who produced it. This rule has been established for at least 90 years."

Efforts to Solve the Problems of Forensic Science Are Already Underway

Tabatha Wethal

Tabatha Wethal is an associate editor at Cygnus Business Media.

Being called infirm, disparate, fragmented, inconsistent and faulty is not exactly a raving review.

But that's what a special committee under the National Academy of Sciences, assigned to review the forensic disciplines and report to U.S. Congress, came back with earlier this year.

It's not as bad as it sounds, though, say forensic experts who testified before the committee in their respective subjects. Much of the report's findings, including calling attention to "fragmentation and inconsistent practices" within forensic science, are not news to those steeped in the industry. Instead, it collectively makes official the reality that within forensics, authorities agree an overhaul is due.

Industry Report Card

In 2007, Congress authorized the National Academy of Sciences to create a committee to review forensic practices nationally. The committee's goal was to assess resource needs of the forensic community and make recommendations on how to further and improve the science and practices behind forensics.

The result of the committee's investigation, its "Strengthening Forensic Science in the United States: A Path Forward"

Tabatha Wethal, "Flawed Forensics?" *Law Enforcement Technology*, July 2009. Copyright © 2009 Cygnus Business Media. All rights reserved. Reproduced by permission.

report, are outlined in the 200-plus page document, serving as a report card on the scientific disciplines with all but DNA analysis coming up short.

The report states, "with the exception of nuclear DNA analysis, however, no forensic method has been rigorously shown to have the capacity to consistently, and with a high degree of certainty, demonstrate a connection between evidence and a specific individual or source."

On first read, that statement could seem rather damning for those working in the nation's nearly 400 forensic crime laboratories. However, industry experts claim the report highlights those disparities that professionals working in forensics know exist.

Max Houck, director of both the forensic lab and forensic science initiatives at West Virginia University, and who also presented on subject matter expertise for the committee in 2007, says the document is a consensus of forensic professional reflection.

What the [National Academy of Sciences] report can do . . . is give law enforcement or forensic professionals a reference when asking for more training and funding.

"It says nothing that hasn't been said in one way or another over the last 20 years," Houck says. "It's just that it came from a much more authoritative source this time."

Carol Henderson, director of the National Clearinghouse for Science, Technology and the Law and a professor of law at Stetson University, regularly speaks at conventions and conferences. Henderson says she agrees with the "Strengthening Forensic Science" report findings.

"Many of the recommendations are already in place, such as accreditation and board certification," Henderson says. "We need to educate people that these efforts are already ongoing. It's not like we're reinventing the wheel here, it's the same thing that's already happening."

What the report can do, Henderson says, is give law enforcement or forensic professionals a reference when asking for more training and funding. It can also serve as the springboard for more research, which Henderson and Houck agree is always welcome. "This can be seen as an opportunity rather than a detriment," Henderson says.

Other Findings

In addition to identifying DNA as the sole sound forensic practice, the report highlights several other areas it considers as "serious problems."

Among other things, the report says:

- ". . . the interpretation of forensic evidence is not always based on scientific studies to determine its validity."

- "These shortcomings obviously pose a continuing and serious threat to the quality of credibility of forensic science practice."

- "The fragmented nature of the forensic science community raises the worrisome prospect that the quality of evidence presented in court . . . can vary unpredictably according to jurisdiction."

And finally:

- "The law's greatest dilemma in its heavy reliance on forensic evidence, however, concerns the question of whether—and to what extent—there is *science* in any given forensic science discipline."

Boiled down to these statements, the report seems to paint a depressing picture of forensics. The panel took in scores of documents and presentations from industry experts and determined that the existing system is flawed. Surprisingly, to a certain degree, forensic experts agree.

"[It] may have been the intent of the committee to jar the community into action," Houck says. "But I think that sort of broad-brush statement, at this juncture, does more damage than it does good. For example, one of my areas is fiber analysis. You have the entirety of the textile science industry behind the analyses that you conduct. So there are standard definitions for nylon, for polyester, for the optical measurements that you make, the dyes, the chemistry, all of this is out there and well characterized, so to say there's no science behind this is a misperception of what that technique is. The broad statement of 'DNA is the only science,' that's troublesome to me."

Forensics authorities say that the people steeped in forensics already know about the problems addressed in the report, and the report just made an official statement of them. Essentially, that none of this was ground-breaking, earth-shattering news for anyone in touch with the industry.

The panel makes several suggestions that would redress and refurbish the current state of forensics. The committee's 13 recommendations, outlined in the report, call for changes such as the creation of a new autonomous entity, which would exclude existing entities; improving and developing graduate programs to attract students to forensic science, strengthening and making lab accreditation mandatory, as well as expert certification; and establish a national forensic code of ethics.

Science Serving the Law

If the report fulfills its goal, to overhaul forensic science, there would be changes to the way forensics are done. The most controversial element involves the proposal that the industry take the crime labs out from law enforcement's hands.

The 13 recommendations the report makes are all based off of its first recommendation: For Congress to establish an independent federal entity, which it tentatively names the National Institute of Forensic Science, to support and oversee forensic science standardization. According to the report, "existing federal entities are too wedded to the current 'fragmented' forensic science community, which is deficient in too many respects." Under the new program, forensic analysis and processes would be removed from working under law enforcement agencies and would instead work independently.

Though the public denouncement of contemporary forensic practices could be seen as negative, those in the industry don't believe it will have a bad effect.

"Science should serve the law," says Harry Edwards, cochair of the committee on Identifying the Needs of the Forensic Science Community, the body authoring the report. In a news conference on the report's release, Edwards explains that establishing autonomous labs would remove human biases and inject more scientific methodologies in forensics.

"Law enforcement shouldn't drive the science," he says. "The scientific enterprise is missing in many of the disciplines here and they need independence to be able to do the work that the committee thinks needs to be done."

Though the public denouncement of contemporary forensic practices could be seen as negative, those in the industry don't believe it will have a bad effect.

Houck has written extensively about forensic science and given presentations on education, business practices and philosophy of forensic science, hairs, fibers and forensic anthropology. In 2007, during the 18 months the committee researched and met with experts from various forensic disciplines, Houck provided information on forensics training and education as well as hair evidence.

"I think the report ... makes some badly needed statements about the industry," Houck says.

Another of the findings referenced poorly trained experts in forensic labs. Houck, who is an instructor and directs educational and professional resources in forensic science, says this finding is valid, adding that there are certain disciplines that have only recently begun to require a bachelor's degree, for example. "There are so few outlets for training that it doesn't surprise me that the committee felt that forensic scientists were overall poorly trained," Houck says. He explains that training is a two-way street: The first part of which there aren't a lot of venues for some training, and two, the laboratories themselves or law enforcement agencies do not have or are able to provide funds for training.

"I wouldn't say it's exactly the fault of the scientists or the profession itself, it's lack of venues and lack of funding," Houck continues. "Considering that people are the greatest expense in a laboratory, you'd want to invest in those people. [Currently] we don't train people like it matters."

Limiting Errors in Justice, Science

Boiled down, the National Academy of Sciences report on the state of forensics may look brutal, but experts immersed in the industry find it accurate and ultimately, necessary that these things be said.

Leaders in the forensics arena like Houck and Henderson remain enthusiastic about the science as a whole, and look forward to building a "better 'forensic science,'" as Henderson puts it. "This is a very exciting time to be in forensic science, I have to say that much," Henderson says.

The study's findings, it is hoped, will help experts put their best foot forward.

The lexis of a German playwright, Bertolt Brecht, from more than a half-century ago sums up the report's resounding message: "The aim of science is not to open the door to infinite wisdom, but to set a limit to infinite error."

The Official Report on the State of Forensics Is Interfering with Prosecutions

Barry Matson

Barry Matson is the deputy director of the Alabama District Attorneys Association and the chief prosecutor for the Alabama Computer Forensic Laboratories.

Mr. Chairman and members of the [Senate Judiciary] Committee, I want to thank you for the honor of appearing before you, to discuss the National Academy of Sciences [NAS] Report, *Strengthening Forensic Sciences in the United States: A Path Forward.* It is especially significant that we appear before you on a subject so vital to the future of law enforcement, prosecution and the administration of justice everywhere.

I am a career prosecutor. My name is Barry Matson. I am the Deputy Director of the Alabama District Attorneys Association and the Chief Prosecutor for the Alabama Computer Forensic Laboratories. Prior to my current position, I was the Chief Deputy District Attorney in Talladega County, Alabama for 16 years. Talladega County is not unlike the vast majority of jurisdictions in America. We were, and are, faced with every manner of drug crime, violent crime, public corruption and gut wrenching homicides. Our trial dockets are growing exponentially. We continually face these challenges with integrity, a strong work ethic, and a deep seeded passion to protect the public and to do justice. Mr. Chairman and members of this committee, we, and no one else, are the only person in the criminal justice system charged with the responsibility of seeking justice. We know, "A prosecutor is held to a higher

Barry Matson, "Testimony to the Senate Committee on the Judiciary, Strengthening Forensic Science in the United States," United States Senate Committee on the Judiciary, September 9, 2009. Reproduced by permission of the author standard than that imposed on other attorneys because of the unique function [we] perform in representing the interest, and exercising the sovereign power, of the state . . ." *People v. Hill.*

In my testimony today I will endeavor to give voice to the 'every day' prosecutor struggling with too few resources, expanding case loads as well as agenda driven criminal defense lobbies. We are also dealing with what we call the "CSI" [*CSI: Crime Scene Investigation* television series] effect, as well as well intended but inexperienced and misguided academicians. We applaud Congress for directing the National Academy of Sciences to undertake the study that led to this report. It is not in spite of the fact we are prosecutors that we welcome a serious critique of the forensic science process, it is because we are prosecutors. But like many endeavors, those with agendas have made an impact not only on this report, but now on courtrooms all over this nation.

Prosecutors and forensic science professionals do more to free the innocent and safeguard the liberties of our citizens than any defense project or academician will accomplish in a career.

The NAS Failed to Consult Prosecutors

The absence of prosecutors on the National Academy of Sciences Committee on Forensic Sciences has not been lost on those of us serving everyday in the trenches of America's courtrooms. The failure of the Committee to seek the consultation of state and local prosecutors in its 'eight' separate meetings is glaring, and overlooks one of the criminal justice systems most vital elements.

Mr. Chairman, you well know the role of the prosecutor in the American system. As far back as 1816 Courts have said that a prosecutor . . . "is to judge between the people and the government; he [she] is to be the safeguard of the one and the advocate for the rights of the other; he [she] ought not to suffer the innocent to be oppressed or vexatiously harassed, any more than those who deserve prosecution to escape; he [she] is to pursue guilt; he [she] is to protect the innocence; he [she] is the judge of circumstances; and according to their true complexion, to combine the public welfare and the [safety] of the citizens, preserving both and not impairing either; he [she] is to decline the use of individual passions and individual malevolence, when he [she] cannot use them for the advantage of the public; he [she] is to lay hold of them where public justice, in sound discretion, requires it" *Fouts v. State.*

The NAS [National Academy of Sciences] report before you seems to erroneously focus upon perceived biases in the forensic and law enforcement communities.

Even though, as a prosecutor, I am part of the executive branch of government, I stand in the gap between the citizen and his or her government. Make no mistake about it; I am, like my colleagues, a tough prosecutor and I vigorously seek justice for the victim and the community. However, that toughness is tempered with honesty, fairness and a simple desire to do what is right.

Mr. Chairman, one thing that has been grossly overlooked in all of this process is the fact that prosecutors and forensic science professionals do more to free the innocent and safeguard the liberties of our citizens than any defense project or academician will accomplish in a career. Those entities have no burden or have taken no oath to seek the truth. Conversely, they are required to suppress the truth when it serves the best interest and needs of their client.

Have regrettable incidences occurred in the forensic setting? Yes. Is it to the level that some entities and special projects would have us believe? Absolutely not. As long as human beings are involved we will endeavor to do the very best we can, but no system will be perfect. However, the NAS report before you seems to erroneously focus upon perceived biases in the forensic and law enforcement communities. Forensic technicians and scientists are said to be rife with cognitive bias. This report says they demonstrate this bias by ignoring base rate information in seeking to please supervisors, or by basing results on suggested questions or how the data is presented. Some passages suggest that forensic scientists might simply see 'things' that do not exists, and that they skew the outcome of cases by intentionally presenting their findings in an unfair way to produce a particular result. If we are to follow this logic, we must ask this question Mr. Chairman. When a fingerprint examiner tells us that a suspect is excluded as the source of the latent print, should we now charge them anyway because the examiners cognitive bias may have affected the examination? Or when the drug toxicology report tells us the drugs in the possession of the defendant were not controlled, should we assume that they were actually illegal substances and incarcerate the individual? Obviously the answer is a resounding, no. These are silly questions, but they make a point that is overlooked by this report. In other words, this report suggests that the only time forensic sciences is wrong or inaccurate is when the conclusion by the scientist or technician points to the guilt of the accused. If the evidence does not, then everything is okay.

The NAS Report Has Had Negative Impact on Prosecutions

As we speak, in courtrooms in the respective states of all Senators on this Committee, a prosecutor is trying to do the right thing. As a seeker of truth, that prosecutor must be able to take every possible tool into the courtroom. If she does not have the forensic evidence juries have come to expect from a satiation of crime scene television and defense bar demands, she is bludgeoned with pleas of "where are the fingerprints", or "where is the bullet?" If that prosecutor has such evidence, and it is relevant and admissible, she must now defend that evidence from the defense lawyers' attacks using this NAS report.

Mr. Chairman, it is vital that you know the negative impact that this report has already had on prosecutors trying to find the truth. In every jurisdiction across this country, former convictions and current prosecutions are being challenged by using the words of the NAS report to attack forensic science evidence. This is true even though the report made efforts to say that no judgment is made about past convictions and no view is expressed as to whether courts should reassess cases that already have been tried. But the report went on to say, [However] . . . there are serious issues regarding the capacity and quality of the current forensic science system; yet, the courts continue to rely on forensic evidence. . . . The report concludes that every effort must be made to limit the risk of having the reliability of certain forensic science methodologies judicially certified before the techniques have been properly studied and their accuracy verified. We ask this committee, how could these words not be used to attack prior and current prosecutions where any forensic science discipline has been utilized?

We in the criminal justice arena know that most forensic evidence is rare. None is more rare than fingerprint evidence because they are only 'chance impressions' and the depositing of a latent fingerprint depends on many variables. When we don't have fingerprint evidence, we must constantly counter the defense attack that we have no fingerprint evidence. This defense argument of, "if only we had fingerprints" is heard every day. Now, in the rare cases where we do have fingerprint evidence, we are being faced with the NAS report as defense exhibit number (1).

Mr. Chairman, I feel compelled to address another issue raised by this report that touches on an expertise that I possess as a prosecutor, digital evidence. To give this perspective, two years ago the Alabama District Attorneys Association in conjunction with the US Department of Homeland Security, the US Secret Service, the State of Alabama and others, created the National Computer Forensics Institute, (NCFI). This is the first national institution dedicated exclusively to the training of state and local law enforcement, prosecutors and judges in all areas of digital evidence in the criminal justice system. In the very short time we have been operational, we have already trained [at no cost to the student] over 600 law enforcement officers, prosecutors and trial judges from 49 different states and Guam and Puerto Rico. In addition, with the help of Alabama's congressional delegation, we began the only state-wide system of computer forensics labs in the United States, known as the Alabama Computer Forensics Laboratories (ACFL). I have been the Chief Prosecutor for the ACFL for the past 4 years and we have tried several hundred cases generated from these types of investigations. The NAS report before you includes the process of preserving and extracting digital evidence under the category of "sciences", when in fact, it is truly more of a methodology employing various computer software.

As an investigative tool, every discipline of forensic sciences has not simply led to a conviction, but has delivered the truth.

Many of the NAS Recommendations Are Already Being Met

The report does make several observations regarding the needs of the digital forensic community. The report says: Three holdover challenges remain: (1) the digital evidence community does not have an agreed certification program or list of qualifications for digital forensic examiners; (2) some agencies still treat the examination of digital evidence as an investigative rather than a forensic activity; and (3) there is wide variability in and uncertainty about the education, experience, and training of those practicing this discipline. I would first make the point that computer forensics or digital forensics is the fastest emerging and one of the most significant tools that law enforcement has in our investigative arsenal. Drug deals are now set up, via text messaging. We are finding web browser searches by murder defendants which demonstrate prior planning of the murder, and how they will kill their victim. We also routinely find emails between bank employees showing their detailed plans to defraud the institution. These are invaluable pieces of evidence to investigators and ultimately to the trier of fact.

As for the training and certification, the NCFI is uniquely situated to fulfill the recommendations of the NAS report. The NCFI was conceived, designed, built and functions solely as a training and education facility for digital evidence. I mention this facility to demonstrate that there are institutions available that are already meeting many of the challenges mentioned in the NAS report.

We welcome the recommendations in the NAS report. We believe that some of these will serve to strengthen forensic sciences for years to come. However, we absolutely recognize and vehemently disagree with the portions that are agenda driven attacks upon well founded investigative techniques. These same techniques or sciences are used everyday to find truth in every type of case. As an investigative tool, every discipline of forensic sciences has not simply led to a conviction, but has delivered the truth. I know this truth, and I sleep very well at night knowing that dedicated prosecutors, forensic technicians and scientists working in independent or law enforcement

Forensic Technology Has Been Wrongly Criticized as Unscientific

Crime Lab Report

Crime Lab Report is an independent organization that analyzes media coverage, public policy trends, and current issues affecting the profession of forensic science.

Michael J. Saks of Arizona State University and David L. Faigman of the University of California at San Francisco have become increasingly effective advocates for what they argue is a better brand of forensic science. From their perspective, the pattern identification disciplines such as those involving the identification of latent prints, firearms & toolmarks, and shoe impressions do not meet the standards to which they argue *real* science must conform.

A blistering critique titled "Failed Forensics: How Forensic Science Lost its Way and How it Might Yet Find It," was published by Saks and Faigman in July 2008 in the *Annual Review of Law and Social Science*. In their words, pattern identification disciplines "have little or no basis in actual science. They neither borrow from established science nor systematically test their hypotheses."

As a courtesy to our readers, here is a quick peek at some of the claims that appeared in the aforementioned article:

- "The nonscience forensic sciences . . . are scientific failures in the sense that science . . . played little more than a rhetorical part in the development of these fields."

"Forensic Pattern Identification: A History Lesson, and Some Advice, for Saks and Faigman," Crime Lab Report, January 21, 2009. Copyright © 2009 by Crime Lab Report. All rights reserved. Reproduced by permission.

- "Absent any testing that can be replicated by other researchers and independently verified by courts, forensic identification science is not really a science at all."

- "Although knowledge from organic chemistry can be brought to bear in identifying what drugs, poisons, or medications might be discovered in a corpse found at a crime scene, what knowledge from conventional sciences like biology or chemistry or physics support the notion of individualization."

- "Most of the forensic identification sciences, however, missed the school bus. They never joined the university system. . . . They became an instrument of law enforcement, largely controlled by police technicians and their superiors."

- "If forensic individualization science had emerged from normal science, its approach and its techniques probably would resemble DNA typing, with its measurement of attributes, sampling of variation in populations, and statistical bases.". . .

Evidence of Research in Forensic Science Is Available

Crime Lab Report is troubled by Professors Saks' and Faigman's failure to do due diligence in their review of the available literature. If they are unhappy with the fact that they could not find the evidence of research and scholarly review that they would expect, we would politely argue that they should have looked a bit harder. The evidence they seek cannot be found in the *New York Times*, legal journals, or papers written by misguided academicians who have joined the chorus of forensic science critics hoping to bring attention to themselves and their universities. . . .

Even the slightest bit of effort would have allowed Saks and Faigman to find and summarize the groundbreaking work sponsored by the *Midwest Forensic Resource Center (MFRC)* at the Ames Laboratory, which is operated for the U.S. Department of Energy by Iowa State University. Research investigators including Christophe Champod at the University of Lausanne in Switzerland are systematically invalidating claims by critics, including Michael Saks, that contextual bias in latent print verifications tends to corrupt the results of forensic examiners.

In fact, it appears that the research may show the exact opposite to be true. According to a research and development program summary published by the *MFRC* in October 2008:

> ... fingerprint experts under the biasing conditions provided significantly fewer definitive and erroneous conclusions than the control group. They tended to provide opinions that were inconclusive.

> Novice participants were more influenced by the bias conditions and did tend to make incorrect judgments, especially when prompted towards an incorrect response by the bias prompt. This was not the case with the fingerprint experts.

The public suffers immeasurably when activism is fraudulently packaged and presented as scholarly research.

The results of this research have been presented at national and international conferences, Therefore, *Crime Lab Report* can only speculate why Saks and Faigman either missed it entirely or simply did not follow their own advice when they argued that good research must "maximize the contribution of the phenomenon under scrutiny and minimize the contribution of expectations and biases."

Critics of Forensic Technology Ignore Evidence to Promote Social Changes

In our view, Saks and Faigman are simply guilty of using their resources and academic affiliations to promote social changes despite overwhelming factual evidence that invalidates their core arguments.

This kind of behavior is not research nor science. It is activism.

The public suffers immeasurably when activism is fraudulently packaged and presented as scholarly research. But the trend will continue if more qualified professionals and professional organizations aren't willing to take the time or risk to vigorously challenge it. . . .

All science requires that imperfect human beings draw conclusions about what they see and measure.

We would like to offer Saks, Faigman, and other commentators a few valuable lessons that we hope will shape their thinking about disciplines practiced in forensic testing laboratories:

1. If DNA analysts could observe and compare DNA with their own eyes they would do it. Examiners of latent prints, firearm evidence, and toolmarks are fortunate because they can actually observe the evidence in question. They can see the ridge detail of a fingerprint and they can see the striae and impressions on fired bullets and cartridge cases. They don't need instrumental data to tell them what they are looking at. They can see it. They can report it. They can even photograph it. Even better, the analytical processes in these disciplines rarely require them to consume evidence, which makes it available for others to review at a later time.

2. There is no such thing as a purely objective science. All science requires that imperfect human beings draw conclusions about what they see and measure. DNA and chemistry are no exceptions. Even in mathematics, commonly described as the only *pure* science, calculations must be applied to real world problems using careful interpretation and professional judgment. When all subjectivity is eliminated from an endeavor, science is no longer needed because there are no interpretations to govern. Without interpretation, there is no science.

3. Universities do not have a monopoly on science. Science does not require the control and oversight of universities as Saks and Faigman repeatedly emphasized. While universities are highly regarded for their expertise and resources, their focus is more often drawn toward projects that bring notoriety and/or funding.

Science is, and should be, a very inclusive institution that avails itself to any number of people seeking to solve any number of problems. Its fundamental tenets demand that knowledge be gathered in a controlled and systematic way. Then, when it comes time to apply this knowledge, practitioners must exercise professionalism, caution, and self-restraint so that they do not stray beyond what the accumulated knowledge can justify. The forensic laboratory disciplines are very young when compared to other fields. But as long as they continue to advance and provide knowledge that improves the human condition, they are traveling successfully on the path we call science.

4. Until recently, there was no economic justification for universities to invest in forensic research on a large programmatic scale. It wasn't until the early 1960s that epidemic increases in crime necessitated the creation of the large network of crime laboratories that we know today. Furthermore, many of the legal decisions issued by the United States Supreme Court under Chief Justice Earl Warren during the 1950s and 1960s placed an increased emphasis on scientific evidence and a decreased emphasis on information gathered exclusively from police interrogations and suspect confessions. Eventually, with the dawn of the 21st century and demand for services at all-time highs, forensic science funding became more widespread and therefore attracted the attention of many universities (and critics) that had little prior interest in the field.

5. The history of pattern identification and uniqueness is rooted solidly in academics. The most famous pioneers of the pattern identification disciplines had strong academic backgrounds. For example, Calvin Goddard, regarded as the father of firearm identification, was a medical doctor and professor at Northwestern University. He was also the military editor for the *Encyclopedia Britannica*.

Disciplines such as latent print identification and firearm & toolmark identification are reliable, valid, and useful sciences.

Another pioneer in the forensic identification of firearms, Dr. J. Howard Matthews, worked for nearly forty years in the field. Matthews obtained his Master's and Ph.D. from Harvard and served as a professor of chemistry at the University of Wisconsin for over thirty years. He was a fellow of the American Association for the Advancement of Science and one of the founders of the professional chemical fraternity Alpha Chi Sigma. His classic three-volume treatise, *Firearms Identification*, was the largest single source of information on firearms identification ever assembled.

Finally, Sir Francis Galton, a brilliant statistician who demonstrated the uniqueness and permanence of fingerprints, conducted research at Trinity College and the University of Cambridge. He was instrumental in developing methods for studying variations in the human population, which ultimately fueled the growth of latent print identification as we know it.

6. The innocent are protected by the pattern identification disciplines. If allowed to go unchecked, Saks' and Faigman's zeal for activism would actually harm the innocent. Firearm examiners, for example, frequently identify firearms that were *not* used in the commission of crimes. Similarly, latent print examiners are more likely to exclude individuals as viable suspects than to include them. Therefore, the tendency of activists to portray forensic science as being reserved for the demonstration of guilt ignores the value of pattern evidence in preventing the wrongful arrest and/or conviction of innocent persons.

So here are the facts. Disciplines such as latent print identification and firearm & toolmark identification are reliable, valid, and useful sciences. They are bodies of knowledge and applied methods that have developed over a long period of time during which many competent researchers attempted to falsify their underlying hypotheses and failed.

Certainly, continuing research and improvement must be a constant force in the evolution of all forensic disciplines. But critics who have committed themselves to lowering public confidence in our criminal justice system are choosing to ignore compelling evidence at the expense of public safety. For this alone their tactics and rhetoric should be repudiated.

Saks and Faigman complain that there is insufficient research to support the conclusions rendered by pattern identification experts. Then why can't they present research (preferably that which meets their stated standards of validity) that demonstrates such conclusions to be unreliable?

Because it doesn't exist.

When the proper methods are used and the appropriate quality-assurance checks are employed, the subsequent results in the pattern identification disciplines can be reported with a degree of confidence that makes them useful to the criminal justice system.

The Real Problem in Forensics Is Poor Wording of Conclusions

This leads us into what we believe is the real issue that Saks and Faigman are trying to address but are too distracted by their own biases and expectations to take notice of.

Crime Lab Report believes that the single most serious technical problem in forensic testing laboratories today is not invalid methods nor lack of research. It is poorly and ambiguously worded conclusions that leave laypersons with an incomplete or confused understanding of what the results actually mean.

This problem has *nothing* to do with the validity or admissibility of a science and can often be mitigated with some simple questioning. But it does represent a sort of malpractice that should not be tolerated by the forensic laboratory community nor its stakeholders.

In the forensic testing sciences, a particularly heavy burden is placed on practitioners to report clear and complete conclusions that are unlikely to be misconstrued. If the wrong words are used or if poor writing skills preclude the reader from understanding the meaning of a testing report, even the most reliable science can be made to look suspicious or even inferior.

Too often, laboratory directors and quality-control managers struggling with overflowing backlogs and shoestring budgets don't provide solid training to scientists in the areas of courtroom testimony and technical writing. Other labs are simply hesitant to change the status quo and prefer to stick with the language to which they have become accustomed. As a result, they inappropriately prioritize the preservation of tradition at the expense of scientific clarity.

Perhaps evidenced by the criticisms of Saks and Faigman, these weaknesses seem to bear heavily on practitioners in the pattern identification disciplines which necessarily rely upon direct observation instead of instrumental analysis. Pattern identification experts would be wise to carefully review and standardize the wording of their conclusions to eliminate ambiguity and maximize scientific value. We believe the right changes would drastically empower these embattled disciplines and better serve their stakeholders.

The forensic science community has worked tirelessly and successfully to improve its administrative and technical practices through accreditation, certification, and more comprehensive methods for managing quality. We know this progress will continue. *Crime Lab Report* believes, however, that better and more consistent wording of conclusions is a new frontier that forensic practitioners will embark on in the next several years. By doing so, they will make it harder for critics like Saks and Faigman to confuse weak communication skills for scientific invalidity.

We would like to believe that Michael Saks and David Faigman are intelligent men who want our criminal justice system to be accurate and fair. But their publications reveal a systemic ignorance and carelessness that will only inhibit their ability to make a positive and lasting impact on the criminal justice system.

It's up to them to decide if they want to be activists or genuine truth-seekers.

We advise the latter.

CHAPTER 2

Does the "*CSI* Effect" Influence Verdicts in Jury Trials?

Chapter Preface

Almost everyone has heard of the television drama *CSI: Crime Scene Investigation*, and many people watch it regularly. As of 2006, it was estimated that more than sixty million viewers were seeing one or more of the *CSI* episodes every week. There are also other crime series that have appeared in response to its popularity. Before *CSI*, the general public knew little or nothing about forensic technology and was not very interested in it. The show has changed that. It has even led to a large increase in the number of students preparing for careers in forensic science.

But the way television portrays forensics is far from realistic. "Watch an episode of *CSI*," wrote Jeffrey Kluger in the October 21, 2002, issue of *Time* magazine, "and you would think forensic investigators move in a world of lab coats fresh from the cleaners, offices done up in glass brick and autopsy tables artfully—and pointlessly—underlit in purple. The fact is that in communities in which forensic labs compete for funds from the same pot of money out of which beat cops are paid, there's no room for such luxuries. Even gadgets like the mass spectrometers get snazzed up for TV, with flashing lights and screen images that simply don't exist. . . . Most criminal cases don't get cracked overnight. On TV, however, investigators have less than an hour to go from crime to capture, so time lines get dramatically—sometimes preposterously—compressed."

Kluger went on to say, "The myth of quick-and-easy crime busting may be starting to get in the way of law enforcement. Forensic scientists speak of something they call the *CSI* effect, a growing public expectation that police labs can do everything TV labs can. This, they worry, may poison jury pools, which could lose the ability to appreciate the shades of gray that color real criminal cases." His statement was the first mention of the *CSI* effect in print. Since then, there have been dozens of articles dealing with it, along with many scholarly papers.

Most of the concern has been expressed by prosecutors, who say that because people have become used to seeing sophisticated forensic technology solve fictional crimes, juries now have similar expectations in real cases and refuse to convict defendants in trials that lack such evidence. When prosecutors fail to present such evidence, they say, juries are not convinced by strong non-forensic evidence, such as eyewitness statements and sometimes even admissions of guilt by the defendent. Many legal experts believe this to be true. Others, however, have argued that familiarity with *CSI* ought to work in the opposite way—it should favor prosecutors because people have been led to assume that the forensic evidence, on which arrests are based, is more reliable than it actually is.

There is no statisical proof that the *CSI* effect is influencing verdicts, and the extent of its impact on juries is a controversial issue. However, whether or not it influences juror behavior, it definitely influences attorney behavior. Prosecutors are pressuring the police to provide more forensic evidence than they otherwise would, and when there is none, they are explaining to juries why it cannot be obtained or was not needed. Defense attorneys are pointing out lack of forensic evidence even, or perhaps especially, when they know the case against the defendant can be made without it. Some judges are allowing attorneys to question prospective jurors about what they watch on television and exclude those who are *CSI* fans. So courtroom tactics will never be quite the same as they were in the era before juries considered themselves informed about forensics.

The TV Drama *CSI* Is Affecting How Jurors React in Real-Life Trials

Richard Willing

Richard Willing is a reporter for USA Today.

Like viewers across the nation, folks in Galveston, Texas, watch a lot of TV shows about crime-scene investigators. Jury consultant Robert Hirschhorn couldn't be happier about that.

Hirschhorn was hired last year [2003] to help defense attorneys pick jurors for the trial of Robert Durst, a millionaire real estate heir who was accused of murdering and dismembering a neighbor, Morris Black. It was a case in which investigators never found Black's head. The defense claimed that wounds to the head might have supported Durst's story that he had killed Black in self-defense.

Hirschhorn wanted jurors who were familiar with shows such as *CSI: Crime Scene Investigation* to spot the importance of such a gap in the evidence. That wasn't difficult: In a survey of the 500 people in the jury pool, the defense found that about 70% were viewers of CBS' *CSI* or similar shows such as Court TV's *Forensic Files* or NBC's *Law & Order*.

Durst was acquitted in November [2003]. To legal analysts, his case seemed an example of how shows such as *CSI* are affecting action in courthouses across the USA by, among other things, raising jurors' expectations of what prosecutors should produce at trial.

Richard Willing, "'CSI Effect' Has Juries Wanting More Evidence," *USA Today*, August 5, 2004. Copyright © 2004 USA Today. Reproduced by permission.

Prosecutors, defense lawyers and judges call it "the *CSI* effect," after the crime-scene shows that are among the hottest attractions on television. The shows—*CSI* and *CSI: Miami*, in particular—feature high-tech labs and glib and gorgeous techies. By shining a glamorous light on a gory profession, the programs also have helped to draw more students into forensic studies.

Real crime-scene investigators say that because of the programs, people often have unrealistic ideas of what criminal science can deliver.

Fostering Unrealistic Ideas

But the programs also foster what analysts say is the mistaken notion that criminal science is fast and infallible and always gets its man. That's affecting the way lawyers prepare their cases, as well as the expectations that police and the public place on real crime labs. Real crime-scene investigators say that because of the programs, people often have unrealistic ideas of what criminal science can deliver.

Like Hirschhorn, many lawyers, judges and legal consultants say they appreciate how *CSI*-type shows have increased interest in forensic evidence.

"Talking about science in the courtroom used to be like talking about geometry—a real jury turnoff," says Hirschhorn, of Lewisville, Texas. "Now that there's this almost obsession with the (TV) shows, you can talk to jurors about (scientific evidence) and just see from the looks on their faces that they find it fascinating."

But some defense lawyers say *CSI* and similar shows make jurors rely too heavily on scientific findings and unwilling to accept that those findings can be compromised by human or technical errors.

Prosecutors also have complaints: They say the shows can make it more difficult for them to win convictions in the large majority of cases in which scientific evidence is irrelevant or absent.

"The lesson that both sides can agree on is, what's on TV does seep into the minds of jurors," says Paul Walsh, chief prosecutor in New Bedford, Mass., and president of the National District Attorneys Association. "Jurors are going to have information, or what they think is information, in mind. That's the new state of affairs."

Prosecutors have begun to ask judges for permission to question prospective jurors about their TV-watching habits.

Lawyers and judges say the *CSI* effect has become a phenomenon in courthouses across the nation:

- In Phoenix [Ariz.] last month [July 2004], jurors in a murder trial noticed that a bloody coat introduced as evidence had not been tested for DNA. They alerted the judge. The tests hadn't been needed because the defendant had acknowledged being at the murder scene. The judge decided that TV had taught jurors about DNA tests, but not enough about when to use them.

- Three years ago in Richmond, Va., jurors in a murder trial asked the judge whether a cigarette butt found during the investigation could be tested for links to the defendant. Defense attorneys had ordered DNA tests but had not yet introduced them into evidence. The jury's hunch was correct—the tests exonerated the defendant, and the jury acquitted him.

- In Arizona, Illinois and California, prosecutors now use "negative evidence witnesses" to try to assure jurors that it is not unusual for real crime-scene investigators to fail to find DNA, fingerprints and other evidence at crime scenes.

- In Massachusetts, prosecutors have begun to ask judges for permission to question prospective jurors about their TV-watching habits. Several states already allow that.

- Last year in Wilmington, Del., federal researchers studying how juries evaluate scientific evidence staged dozens of simulated trials. At one point, a juror struggling with especially complicated DNA evidence lamented that such problems never come up "on *CSI*."

The *CSI* effect also is being felt beyond the courtroom.

At West Virginia University, forensic science is the most popular undergraduate major for the second year in a row, attracting 13% of incoming freshmen this fall [2004]. In June, supporters of an Ohio library drew an overflow crowd of 200-plus to a luncheon speech on DNA by titling it "CSI: Dayton."

The Los Angeles County Sheriff's Department crime lab has seen another version of the *CSI* effect. Four technicians have left the lab for lucrative jobs as technical advisers to crime-scene programs. "They found a way to make science pay," lab director Barry Fisher says.

Shows' Popularity Soars

CSI, which begins its fifth season next month [September 2004], was America's second-most-popular TV program during the season that began last fall, after the Tuesday edition of *American Idol*.

CSI and a spinoff, *CSI: Miami* (which is about to begin its third season), have drawn an average of more than 40 million viewers a week during the past TV season. *Law & Order*, whose plots sometimes focus on forensic evidence, has been the 13th-most-watched show during the 2003–04 season, averaging about 15 million viewers. On cable, the Discovery Channel, A&E and Court TV have programs that highlight DNA testing or the analysis of fingerprints, hair and blood-spatter patterns.

CSI: NY, set in New York City, is slated to premiere next month.

The *CSI* shows combine whiz-bang science with in-your-face interrogations to solve complex crimes. Some sample dialogue from actor David Caruso, the humorless monotone who plays investigator Horatio Caine on *CSI: Miami*: "He (the bad guy) doesn't know how evidence works, but you know what? He will."

The shows' popularity, TV historians say, is partly a result of their constant presence. Counting network and cable, at least one hour of crime-forensics programming airs in prime time six nights a week.

The stars of the shows often are the equipment—DNA sequencers, mass spectrometers, photometric fingerprint illuminators, scanning electron microscopes. But the technicians run a close second.

"It's 'geek chic,' the idea that kids who excel in science and math can grow up to be cool," says Robert Thompson, who teaches the history of TV programming at Syracuse University. "This is long overdue.... Cops and cowboys and doctors and lawyers have been done to death."

Departing from Reality

Some of the science on *CSI* is state-of-the-art. Real lab technicians can, for example, lift DNA profiles from cigarette butts, candy wrappers and gobs of spit, just as their Hollywood counterparts do.

But some of what's on TV is far-fetched. Real technicians don't pour caulk into knife wounds to make a cast of the weapon. That wouldn't work in soft tissue. Machines that can identify cologne from scents on clothing are still in the experimental phase. A criminal charge based on "neuro-linguistic programming"—detecting lies by the way a person's eyes shift—likely would be dismissed by a judge.

But real scientists say *CSI*'s main fault is this: The science is always above reproach. "You never see a case where the sample is degraded or the lab work is faulty or the test results don't solve the crime," says Dan Krane, president and DNA specialist at Forensic Bioinformatics in Fairborn, Ohio. "These things happen all the time in the real world."

Defense lawyers say the misconception that crime-scene evidence and testing are always accurate helps prosecutors. "Jurors expect the criminal justice system to work better than it does," says Betty Layne DesPortes, a criminal defense lawyer in Richmond, Va., who has a master's degree in forensic science.

She notes that during the past 15 years, human errors and corruption have skewed test results in crime labs in West Virginia, Pennsylvania, California, Texas and Washington state.

But prosecutors say the shows help defense lawyers. Jurors who are regular viewers, they say, expect testable evidence to be present at all crime scenes.

In fact, they say, evidence such as DNA and fingerprints—the staple of *CSI* plots—is available in only a small minority of cases and can yield inconclusive results.

"Defense attorneys will get up there and bang the rail and say 'Where were the DNA tests?' to take advantage of the idea that's in the juror's mind," says Joshua Marquis, a prosecutor in Astoria, Ore. "You've got to do a lot of jury preparation to defeat that."

Some prosecutors have gone to great lengths to lower jurors' expectations about such evidence.

In Belleville, Ill., last spring, prosecutor Gary Duncan called on seven nationally recognized experts to testify about scientific evidence against a man accused of raping and murdering a 10-year-old girl. The witnesses included specialists in human and animal DNA, shoe-print evidence, population statistics and human mitochondrial DNA, genetic material that is inherited only from one's mother and that seldom is used in criminal cases. Duncan won a conviction.

"I wanted to be certain the jury was clear on the evidence and its meaning," he says. "These days, juries demand that."

CSI producers acknowledge that they take some liberties with facts and the capabilities of science, but they say it's necessary to keep their story lines moving.

Elizabeth Devine, a former crime lab technician who writes and produces episodes of *CSI: Miami,* spoke at a training seminar for prosecutors last year in Columbia, S.C. She said that if the shows did not cut the time needed to perform DNA tests from weeks to minutes, a villain might not be caught before "episode five."

For all of *CSI*'s faults, some lab technicians say they have a soft spot for the TV version of their world. "It's great for getting people interested (in) careers" in forensic science, says Barbara Llewellyn, director of DNA analysis for the Illinois State Police.

Terry Melton, president of Mitotyping Technologies in State College, Pa., says the programs have made "jury duty something people now look forward to."

And Fisher says the shows have given "science types" like himself some unexpected cachet.

"When I tell someone what I do, I never have to explain it now," he says. "They know what a crime-scene (technician) does. At least, they think they do."

The *CSI* Effect Is Leading to Unwarranted Acquittals

Jeffrey Heinrick

At the time this viewpoint was written, Jeffrey Heinrick was a police investigator in Phoenix, Arizona. He is now a law student.

The *CSI* effect can best be described as a phenomenon where television "educated" jurors are more likely to not convict someone who is guilty because procedures and techniques they observed from the fictional television show [*CSI: Crime Scene Investigation*] were not applied in the case. Max Houck, Director of the Forensic Science Initiative at West Virginia University, says "The *CSI* effect is basically the perception of the near-infallibility of forensic science in response to the TV show". The *CSI* effect is a recent phenomenon that can be attributed to the influence of mass media. The term started appearing in legal lexicon in 2003; roughly 3 years after the show and its spin-offs became wildly popular television options for the American public.

It is estimated that over 60 million people watch the *CSI* television shows every week. There is another unexpected side effect from the television series; there has been a huge increase in forensic sciences undergraduate students at universities across the United States. For example, West Virginia University graduated 4 Forensic Science undergrads in 1999. In 2004, that number shot up to 400. Now [2006], there are at least 90 forensic science programs at universities all over the United States. Last year, 180 people applied for 20 graduate position spots at Michigan State University; the field has become extremely competitive.

Juries are broken down into two forms, petite and grand. A petite jury has at least 6 jurors, and deals mostly in cases

Jeffrey Heinrick, "Everyone's an Expert: The CSI Effect's Negative Impact on Juries," *Triple Helix*, Fall 2006, pp. 59–61. Copyright © 2006 The Triple Helix. All rights reserved. Reproduced by permission.

that involve misdemeanors. Grand juries have 12 jurors and deal with offenses that are felonies. Of course there are exceptions to this rule based on different local jurisdictions, but for the most part, this is the standard of the American legal system. In America, a vast majority of criminal cases are settled by plea bargain. In the rare circumstance that a case requires a jury, such cases are often sensationalized by the media and are portrayed as occurring more frequently than the true incidence rate.

Juries Demand Forensic Evidence

Recent high-profile cases that were decided by jury, such as the [actor] Robert Blake and [singer/entertainer] Michael Jackson trials, rely not on the fact that either the prosecutor or defense will make a better case, but rather on the ambiguity and uncertainty on the part of an uninformed jury. Juries like these are more likely to fall back on what they know and feel comfortable with—evidentiary procedures they have viewed on television. In the Robert Blake murder trial, the jury voted to acquit him. The question of the *CSI* effect was raised in Robert Blake's acquittal. The prosecution felt that it had a strong case against Robert Blake. His alibi was that he "left his gun in the car", went to collect it, and found his wife with a bullet in her head. There was also sworn testimony that Mr. Blake had tried to hire someone to kill his wife and openly discussed having her killed. The prosecution felt that even though the physical evidence was lacking, the witness testimony and the odd behavior of Mr. Blake himself was damning.

The jury, however, needed the hard evidence. Due to a lack of gun shot residue and blood on his clothes, the jury voted to acquit Robert Blake. The Los Angeles district attorney in charge of prosecuting him called the jurors "incredibly stupid". It is rare for an attorney to publicly criticize the jurors, but in this case, his frustration is understood. The district attorney firmly believes that the *CSI* effect was involved in the jury's decision to acquit Mr. Blake.

This is not the first time that the *CSI* effect has been blamed in an acquittal where the prosecution felt that they had an extremely strong case:

Jurors now demand expensive and often unnecessary DNA tests, handwriting analyses, gun shot residue testing, and other procedures that are not pertinent to the case.

An Illinois man was accused of the attempted murder of his estranged girlfriend. The jury acquitted him because the police didn't test the blood stained bed sheets for DNA. After being released from jail for a parole violation, he immediately found his ex girlfriend and stabbed her to death. In Baltimore [Md.], a man was acquitted of murder despite the fact that there were two eyewitnesses to the shooting. The prosecution blames the *CSI* effect because the jury wouldn't go on witness testimony alone; they wanted more rigorous testing of physical evidence. . . .

These are not uncommon examples of the *CSI* effect on cases. Jurors now demand expensive and often unnecessary DNA tests, handwriting analyses, gun shot residue testing, and other procedures that are not pertinent to the case. This poses a problem for both the prosecution and defense sides of a trial case. These procedures are often extremely expensive and time consuming. Crime labs are already backed up to full capacity, often waiting months, or even years to provide tangible evidence. In the case of Richard Ramirez, AKA the Night Stalker, forensic scientists spent two years carefully analyzing and interpreting the evidence. Many juries do not understand that this type of analysis takes time, money, and patience.

A recent study done by the Maricopa County [Ariz.] Attorney's Office (MCAO) conducted a survey of 102 prosecutors with jury trial experience. They were asked about their personal experiences with juries who exhibited signs of the *CSI* Effect. The study conducted by the MCAO concluded that the *CSI* effect was a "significant influence" on Maricopa County juries. The MCAO is one of the biggest prosecutorial bodies in the United States, so it is not a far leap to imagine that the *CSI* Effect is present in larger cities, such as New York, Los Angeles, and Chicago.

While Star Trek *influenced a generation of scientists, physicists, and inventors, the* CSI *shows are potentially influencing jury trials where people's lives are at stake.*

Television Shows Have Strong Influence

Television has influenced society in many ways since its inception. A recent airing of a show on the History Channel called *How William Shatner Changed the World* explored in great detail how today's society has been influenced by the original series of *Star Trek*. Our modern devices like extremely compact cell phones and MRIs [magnetic resonance imaging scanners] are analogous to the Communicator and the Biobed. Television shows and mass media bring an expectation that people should have these types of things and procedures available to them, despite the feasibility of the invention. While *Star Trek* influenced a generation of scientists, physicists, and inventors, the *CSI* shows are potentially influencing jury trials where people's lives are at stake.

There is also historical precedent for television's influence on the judicial system. In the 1950's, *Perry Mason* became a very popular television show in America. Every week, he would regularly approach the jury box, make his case directly to them. . . . Before that show, attorneys rarely approached the jury box. By watching this TV show, jurors believed that that kind of behavior from attorneys was normal and expected it. In the 1980's, *The People's Court* with Judge Wapner became very popular. In a 1989 study, researchers determined that this show "increased jurors' expectations of a quick trial, making more jurors frustrated with the length and nuances of real trials".

The show [CSI] . . . often uses technology that is either highly stylized, experimental, or is non-existent.

The *CSI* effect has both its proponents and its detractors. One side argues that it has a completely negative effect on the criminal justice system; while the other is that it is creating better-informed jurors on what is needed to prove that someone is truly guilty. The creator of the *CSI* Television shows, Anthony E. Zuicker, has weighed in on the effect. "The *CSI* effect is, in my opinion, the most amazing thing that has ever come out of the series. For the first time in American History, you're not allowed to fool the jury anymore".

The *CSI* effect is exerting an influence on all parts of the criminal justice system. Both the prosecutors and defense attorneys are feeling the need to be more thorough where they didn't need to be before, despite the fact that the extra effort is usually not needed. According to a recent article in *USA Today*, "some defense lawyers say that *CSI* and similar shows make jurors rely too heavily on scientific findings, and are unwilling to accept that those findings can be compromised by human or technical errors". Prosecutors are also feeling the effect; they say shows can make it more difficult for them to win convictions in the large majority of cases in which scientific evidence is irrelevant or absent. Another problem with the show is that it often uses technology that is either highly stylized, experimental, or is non-existent. Some jurors expect both sides to use this kind of technology, the problem being that most of the times this technology doesn't meet the Frye Standard, a set of procedures used as a benchmark for general acceptance of the way the evidence was tested by the scientific community.

The *CSI* Effect Benefits the Defense

Defense lawyers play on the false idea that crime scene evidence and testing are always accurate. "Jurors expect the criminal justice system to work better than it does" says Betty Layne DesPortes, a criminal defense lawyer. Prosecutors say the effect is helping defense attorneys because jurors who are regular viewers expect testable evidence to be present at all crime scenes. "Prosecutors fear the *CSI* effect with juries because, for example, they wonder, 'Why hasn't everything been tested?' Well in fact, not everything needs to be tested". The *CSI* effect has made their job much harder when it doesn't have to be.

Defense attorneys, on the other hand, benefit because it makes the prosecutor's job more difficult and defense attorneys know that jurors are often lay people with little judicial knowledge. In fact, a judge in New York City said that the city's "district attorneys now have so much influence on grand juries that by and large they could get them to indict a ham sandwich." They rely on people who can be easily swayed to one form or another, hopefully delivering a not guilty verdict for their client. The *CSI* effect tends to work in favor of the defense, since the prosecution has to work that much harder to prove their case. Defense attorneys rely on the naivety and unrealistic expectations of a trial jury to obtain the desired judgment.

Prosecuting attorneys despairingly echo this sentiment. Wendy Murphy, a former prosecutor, says that the *CSI* Effect is absolutely real and an impediment on the criminal justice system. "When *CSI* trumps common sense, then you have a systemic problem. The National District Attorney's Association is deeply concerned about the effect of *CSI*." She has openly criticized the ability of jurors to understand these intricacies.

> "You get jurors who don't have a lot of brain cells asking questions after the case is over about why there weren't any fingerprints on the pillow case. It makes no sense. I actually think one of the problems is we're not screening out these jurors who are way too much under the influence of pop culture programs. They shouldn't be allowed to sit in judgment, frankly".

The long-term consequences of the *CSI* effect will be difficult to predict. Social scientists have always had difficulties making a methodological study of a cultural phenomenon. It is controversial for both the prosecution and defense to claim that the *CSI* effect is to blame for lost cases. Is the *CSI* effect real? The *Yale Law Journal* says that it is, "an accepted reality by virtue of its repeated invocation by the media".

The American criminal justice system has now been active for 225 years; how well will it react to the ever changing face of science and technology? Molecular biology is changing the dynamics of the courtroom. Not only do the defending and prosecuting attorneys have to be familiar with the concepts and procedures of biotechnological methods and equipment, but also with their applications in effectively determining the guilt or innocence of a defendant. Eventually, the technology may become mainstream enough that it will be standard procedure in pre-jury screening to ensure that people understand it, both conceptually and in practice. This could eventually lead to more scientifically educated jurors, rather than the current "television educated" jurors who understand that the technology is there, but do not understand how or when it's used. It is not unreasonable to expect that the *CSI* effect will eventually become a permanent part of courtroom dynamics, and that it may force both the defense and prosecuting attorneys to present a much more scientifically sound and airtight case.

Judges Should Take Steps to Counter *CSI*'s Influence on Jurors

Joshua K. Marquis

Joshua K. Marquis is district attorney of Clatsop County, Oregon. He is a former president of the Oregon District Attorney's Association.

Shows like *CSI* and its spin-offs, *Law & Order* and its spin-offs, *NCIS*, *Cold Case*, *Bones* and other forensic crime programs, depict actors using the most advanced forensic equipment and techniques available to solve crimes. These types of shows are ranked among the top 20 in America. While these shows can be educational concerning forensic science, they are—first and foremost—entertaining fiction. Unfortunately, some viewers think the science, equipment and techniques used on these shows are infallible and readily available to all law enforcement. Because of this, there is evidence that the outcome of some trials (conviction/acquittal) has been based upon a juror and/or juror's unrealistic expectation of being presented with an abundance of forensic evidence that will prove the guilt or innocence of a defendant—far beyond a reasonable doubt. In fact, it seems as if a new standard is being created where jurors will soon expect evidence that will prove *beyond all doubt*, the guilt or innocence of a defendant.

Is the "*CSI* Effect" Having an Impact on Our Criminal Justice System?

Is there really a *CSI* effect? Yes. Prosecutors are increasingly encountering the *CSI* Effect among jurors even when they have strong cases, with eyewitnesses and confessions by defen-

Joshua K. Marquis, "CSI Effect—Does It Really Exist?" National District Attorneys Association, October 16, 2007. Copyright © National District Attorneys Association. All rights reserved. Reproduced by permission of the publisher and author.

dants. If they don't have forensic evidence there have been jurors who will not convict a defendant even if no such evidence was available, and the defendant was caught "red-
handed." When these defendants are found "not guilty"
because of the *CSI* Effect and a juror/jurors blind faith and
belief in the truth of popular forensic crime shows—they are
released back into society to continue in their life of crime.
Many of the cases in which juries demand *CSI* level evidence
are often less serious cases, and therefore they rarely make the
news.

How much forensic evidence is enough? There are even
cases where prosecutors present the results of DNA evidence
which positively proves that the defendant committed the
crime, beyond a reasonable doubt. But, a juror may have seen
a forensic crime show where there was more evidence than
DNA. For example, in the show there may have been carpet
fibers from a criminal's home—or other materials from a
crime scene were found on the victim. The juror(s) may insist
that more evidence should have been tested, even if virtually
none existed. These types of juror expectations have resulted
in finding defendants not guilty—even with irrefutable DNA
test results. Ironically, some of these tests are really only valuable to give opinions about whether fibers or hair are consistent with a particular theory. But, based on what juror(s) see
on TV, they expect an expert to give an opinion with certainty, when that is not possible with that kind of evidence.

---

*Most state forensic labs . . . don't have the resources to
match what audiences see being used on the* CSI *and
other forensic crime shows.*

Do TV forensic crime shows include technology that is
questionable or not readily available? Yes. Some jurors expect
certain scientific technology to be available because they've
seen it used on a TV forensic crime show. In many instances,

this is used to create a "WOW—I didn't know that" factor. Because these shows are "entertainment" they may include highly advanced or experimental scientific technology to make the show more interesting. Some of the technology shown on TV may exist somewhere, but often only in research labs or in a few very advanced and sophisticated laboratories. The technology may well exist, but not in many jurisdictions.

How does an actual crime lab compare to those depicted in forensic crime shows? Some jurors may believe that all state forensic laboratories are as well equipped with the most advanced technology as they see in *CSI Las Vegas, Miami* and *New York*—and other forensic crime shows. This could not be further from the truth. Some of this advanced equipment is cost-prohibitive in many cities and states. While most state forensic labs make every effort to keep up-to-date on technological advancements and improved equipment, they don't have the resources to match what audiences see being used on the *CSI* and other forensic crime shows.

For example, how long does it realistically take to get results of forensic tests like DNA, etc.? Unlike the shows on TV, results of DNA and other forensic tests can not be available within the blink of an eye, an hour, a day, or even weeks. This just does not happen! First, DNA and many other test results take much longer in real life, and second, many state crime labs have such a backlog that it can take several months, or longer, to receive results from evidence sent to be tested. It's certainly understandable that a TV writer needs an ending to the show in 45 minutes, and few viewers would watch eight episodes just to find out a DNA result. But, in reality that is, in many instances, just about how long it would take to get those results.

Have forensic crime shows caused an increase in the number and type(s) of evidence being tested? Yes. The fact is that because of these forensic crime shows there now exists a much higher bar for police and prosecutors to reach in proving the guilt of defendants. Expensive tests are run on evidence such as fingerprints, DNA, etc.—even when the defendant was "caught in the act" of committing the crime for which he/she is being tried by police and eye-witnesses.

How Are Attorneys Responding to the *CSI* Effect?

Are defense attorneys using the *CSI* effect to their advantage? Yes. They do so by letting the jury know when prosecutors have little or no forensic evidence available to convict their client. They are telling the jury, that without hard forensic evidence—there can be no proof that their defendant is guilty. Defense attorneys claim the *CSI* Effect is a good thing because it places a higher standard for investigators. Yet, jurors should never forget that the defense attorney's job is to sow doubt whether it really exists or not.

Prosecutors are using . . . (the jury selection process) to weed-out "True Believers" in the infallibility of TV forensic crime shows.

How can, and are, prosecutors responding to the *CSI* Effect? If evidence exists, but there is a question as to the need to have it tested, within reason, prosecutors are doing so anyway. When in doubt about what evidence needs to be tested, it is important to anticipate the *CSI* Effect on potential juror questions. Then, by using their best judgment, and recognizing the fact that many forensic labs have backlogs of evidence and are pushed to their limits—make their decision concerning the evidence they want to have tested. A study conducted by the Maricopa County Attorney in Arizona found that, "More than 61% of Arizona prosecutors who ask jurors if they watch forensic crime TV shows feel jurors 'seem to believe the shows are mostly true.'" One prosecutor said, "I have been asking to have evidence submitted for fingerprints and

DNA on a regular basis, sometimes even with admissions of guilt, just to show the jury we are all doing our jobs."

Prosecutors are using Voir Dire (the jury selection process) to weed-out "True Believers" in the infallibility of TV forensic crime shows. During *voir dire*, or the jury selection process, prosecutors are asking jurors if they watch *CSI* and other forensic crime shows. They are also asking if a juror believes what they see on these shows is mostly entertainment—or largely based on fact. Prosecutors can then better determine who to *strike* or eliminate, from becoming a member of the jury based on the probable high expectation by such candidates for a large amount of forensic evidence.

Prosecutors are educating the jury concerning when forensic testing is—and is not—needed. Prosecutors are making every effort to explain to jurors why certain types of evidence was not available or—if available—was not tested. They work with the police, detectives and outside experts to help educate the jury about evidence that is, or is not, available in cases, and explain the importance of such evidence. Prosecutors are also clarifying why eyewitnesses and being caught while committing a crime would negate the need for forensic testing.

Prosecutors are using opening and closing statements to let jurors know what to expect concerning forensic evidence during a trial. In opening and closing remarks, prosecutors are increasingly explaining to the jury why they do—or don't—have forensic evidence. They are telling the jury what this means, in terms of deciding the guilt or innocence of the defendant.

More judges should instruct jurors to base verdicts *only* on testimony and evidence (if any) presented at the trial—*not* on what they've seen on forensic crime shows. Prosecutors are working with judges to impress upon them the importance of countering the *CSI* Effect. They are stressing the importance of adding language to a judge's jury instructions that warns jurors not to base any of their decisions on what they've seen on TV forensic crime shows but, *only* on the evidence and testimony they heard during the trial. The recent Maricopa County Attorney's report found that, "88% of prosecutors felt that judges rarely address the issue of overcoming the *CSI* Effect." One prosecutor indicated that, "Most judges think it's silly I even address these questions in *voir dire.*" Most people who serve on juries take this responsibility very seriously. They don't want to convict the wrong person, but they feel an equal responsibility to hold defendants they find to be guilty accountable for their actions. If prosecutors talk rationally about the *CSI* effect and why forensic evidence is not needed for a conviction in a specific trial, most jurors will respond in a reasoned and responsible manner. . . .

Positive Aspects to *CSI* and Other Forensic Crime Shows

Among the positive results of forensic crime shows—more people are interested in forensics as a career. Before these shows became popular, there was a shortage of qualified candidates to become forensic technicians, scientists and pathologists. And, while the numerous TV forensic crime shows may somewhat glamorize these positions, many more students entering college are interested in pursuing careers in these heretofore understaffed professions. In fact, it should be noted that people who serve in these positions ought to be the best and the brightest. They have an enormous responsibility within our criminal justice system.

Viewers of these shows do learn about techniques and equipment that are revolutionizing the accuracy with which we can determine who did—or did not—commit a crime. When you have jurors use terms like "mitochondrial DNA"— you have jurors who may take as "gospel" what they see on TV forensic crime shows. However, it's important that you remind jurors to remember that these shows are primarily entertainment. Again, we must take the time to help jurors understand the type of evidence they will be considering during a trial.

Are forensic crime shows making police, prosecutors and other law enforcement officials work harder? In certain cases, yes. The *CSI* Effect may be making police, criminal experts, prosecutors and others do more forensic testing—even when such testing might be unnecessary. Is this a bad thing? From an economical standpoint perhaps, however, there may be instances where additional testing of evidence makes it far easier for the prosecutor to convince the jurors to convict a guilty defendant. But, more testing costs more money. And when there is *no* evidence, but a significant amount of hard facts, and/or trustworthy eyewitnesses who can identify the person who committed a crime, common sense—not TV fantasy and fiction—should prevail. If forensic crime shows like *CSI* had existed before the trial of [former football player, spokesperson and actor] O.J. Simpson, a more forensically educated jury might have seen no way out but to find him—and other defendants of that era—guilty.

> Society will become much more safe as technological advancements continue to be made and there becomes little, if any, doubt about who committed a crime. Prosecutors are strong proponents of any sound technology that helps take the guesswork out of the guilt or innocence of a defendant. A well-educated public is a friend—not a foe—of justice within our criminal justice system. And, it's up to prosecutors to help educate the public to differentiate between fact and fiction.

The Criminal Litigation Process Is Being Altered by Fear of the *CSI* Effect

Tamara F. Lawson

Tamara F. Lawson is an associate professor at St. Thomas University School of Law.

The term "*CSI* Effect," in the context of criminal jury trials, is commonly used to define the impact that viewing fictional criminal investigation shows like *Crime Scene Investigation* ("*CSI*") has upon jurors' real life decision-making processes. The *CSI* Effect has been used to explain unexpected jury verdicts; however, this [viewpoint] coins a new term, the "*CSI* Infection," in order to more appropriately describe the thorough impact that the criminal investigation television pop culture phenomenon has made upon the criminal justice system as a whole. The concept of the *CSI* Infection recognizes the multiple areas that the alleged *CSI* Effect impacts, including areas before the verdict, not just the verdict itself. The entire criminal litigation process is potentially influenced by the fear that the *CSI* Effect has created a population of "*CSI* Infected Jurors" that respond to the criminal case and its evidence in different and unexpected ways. . . . Is it appropriate for prosecutors to change their presentation of evidence to a strategy of defensive prosecution based on the perceived fear of *CSI* Infected Jurors? Does it lower the government's burden of proof when the court or the prosecution tells the jury that the case does not have to be proven with *CSI*-type evidence? Is it appropriate to ask a testifying crime scene analyst if his job is like *CSI*? Can litigants make reference to *CSI* during

Tamara F. Lawson, "Before the Verdict and Beyond the Verdict: The CSI Infection within Modern Criminal Jury Trials," *Loyola University Chicago Law Journal*, vol. 41, 2009, pp. 121–26, 128–34, 166–73. Copyright © 2009 Loyola University Chicago, School of Law. Reproduced by permission of the author.

voir dire [jury selection], opening statement, or closing argument? Can a cross-examination or closing argument be curtailed by the court due to fears that *CSI* Infected Jurors will misconstrue certain evidence or argument? Are new and special jury instructions needed to explain the law as well as the task of fact finding to the modern jury—a potentially *CSI* Infected jury? Is it appropriate to ask prospective jurors about their television viewing habits? Correspondingly, is it valid to excuse a juror from serving because he or she watches too many crime shows on television?

These are the types of substantive legal questions that the courts must consider in the age of the *CSI* Infection. . . .

Judges must institute procedural safeguards to combat the CSI *Infection's potential to derail a fair trial.*

Every criminal defendant is entitled to a fair trial. This Sixth Amendment constitutional right is inextricably linked to the analysis of the *CSI* Infection and its impact upon criminal prosecutions. Therefore, this discussion is pivotal to justice. It is imperative for judges to prevent litigants from using tactics that infringe on the fairness of the trial. Moreover, judges must institute procedural safeguards to combat the *CSI* Infection's potential to derail a fair trial. If ignored, the *CSI* Infection may induce inaccurate verdicts, which then impose upon society a very high cost. When factually guilty violent criminals are acquitted because the jury misinterpreted or improperly weighed the evidence, the safety of the public is compromised. When factually innocent individuals are convicted due to the same type of juror confusion, a more severe injury to society occurs. Both mistakes jeopardize the legitimacy of the criminal justice system. However, wrongful convictions are inherently more repugnant to justice.

Some scholarly observers and experts criticize the entire theory and doubt the existence of the *CSI* Effect. Critics highlight the lack of empirical data supporting the conclusion that television shows actually impact jurors' decisions. Proponents point to jurors' statements and illogical, or surprising verdicts as sufficient evidence to prove that the *CSI* Effect is real and worthy of remedial attention. Although much is made of the debate about the existence of the *CSI* Effect, empirical studies may never fully be able to explain how, and to what extent, the *CSI* Effect influences jurors. Moreover, notwithstanding the fact that scholars can neither affirmatively prove, nor effectively explain away the *CSI* Effect, court pleadings establish that the *CSI* Infection exists within modern criminal litigation. Thus, while debate continues, and more empirical analysis is conducted, courtrooms are addressing the issues and the perceived manifestations and mutations of the alleged *CSI* Effect.

The concern for and impact of the *CSI* Effect permeates modern criminal trials. Litigators and judges are forced to deal with it. Motions are based on it, and trial strategies are built around it. Further, judges issue rulings directed at its operation in their real cases and real juries. The *CSI* Infection is now inside the courtroom in a way that can no longer be ignored. . . .

How Crime Shows Mislead Jurors

Jury trials have always required litigants to carefully navigate the delicate psyche of the lay fact-finder. Today, however, a successful trial lawyer must effectively traverse beyond the fixed opinions and pre-judgments that jurors often have before hearing the case. This requires jurors to dislodge themselves from romanticized notions of crime scene investigations and scientific forensic evidence. Instead, jurors must undertake the unfamiliar, perhaps uncomfortable, role of fact-finder, which is a complex job because not every factual question or concern will be answered in a real criminal trial. This is the unpleasant reality of real crimes, the plot is unscripted, and no professional actors deliver the scenes. In order to achieve a just result predicated on realistic and logical inferences from the real case evidence, litigants must overcome the modern juror's heightened expectations and even their misinformation from fictional sources. . . .

Not only have the strategies and arguments of trial lawyers on both sides significantly changed; in fact, trial and appellate courts have also made evidentiary, procedural, and constitutional rulings to address the perceived dangers that *CSI* Infected Jurors impose upon the ultimate fairness of the jury trial process.

Fictional television depictions of criminal investigations and prosecutions are not required to follow the mandatory limitations and requirements imposed by the United States Constitution.

Many anecdotal juror, litigator, and judicial comments reveal that media and popular culture influence jurors' expectations. Some scholars assert that media and culture have always impacted jurors and that the *CSI* television show is no different than science fiction literature, mystery novels, or the *Perry Mason* and *Matlock* television shows. Although it is true these other forms of popular fiction did precede *CSI* and *Law and Order*, the force and scope of the older, more traditional and lower-tech versions of the crime drama never reached the sophistication, popularity, or universal cultural reference of *CSI*. It is almost like asserting that the telegraph and the Internet are essentially the same because they both allow individuals to communicate with each other just like before—nothing has changed. . . . The emergence and popularity of the television shows *Law and Order* and *CSI* tutor the American viewing public in criminal law from a pro-law enforcement vantage point. These shows are purposely skewed for entertainment value and unrestrained by the Federal Rules of Evidence or

Ethical Rules of Professional Conduct. Yet, in real life, the jury is picked from a group of individuals very familiar with the format and content of the fictional version of criminal investigations, evidence gathering, crime solving, and prosecutions. However, these shows fail to present the reality of criminal investigations, such as crime lab backlogs and resource limitations, which real criminal investigators and litigators must surmount. A potential juror's exposure to this distorted version of the prosecutorial process prior to jury service shapes his or her understanding and expectations.

Additionally, fictional television depictions of criminal investigations and prosecutions are not required to follow the mandatory limitations and requirements imposed by the United States Constitution. Real prosecutors are bound by these limitations in order to ensure fairness throughout the entire criminal litigation process. Potentially, these shows sway more than juror expectations; specifically, they may color a juror's analysis of the real evidence presented in court, as well as influence the amount of evidentiary value placed upon certain items of proof. Thus, *CSI* Infected Jurors may have unusually high expectations for the evidence they believe should be presented, and they may have strong opinions regarding the absence of such evidence in trials. Although it is still unclear how alleged heightened expectations and fictional understandings of forensic science are ultimately resolved by each individual jury, one possibility is that information learned from fictional sources, remaining unsatisfied after all the real evidence has been presented, creeps into jury deliberations. . . .

The Age of Defensive Prosecution

Aimed at thwarting the dangers of any potential *CSI* Infection within the jury, many prosecutors have expanded their expert witness lists and requested permission to introduce a broader array of explanatory evidence in their case-in-chief. This type of prosecution strategy is called defensive prosecution. Jurors want to know why certain types of tests were not done, and an explanation regarding the absence of evidence is helpful to overcome any reasonable doubt the jury may have and curb unrealistic expectations and misinformation regarding forensic science and its capabilities. Defensive prosecution also attempts to blunt arguments raised by the defense regarding insufficiency of the evidence.

Defensive prosecutions, however, do not proceed without objection by the defendant. As a counter-tactic to the prosecution's request to admit evidence that explains the investigation and why certain scientific evidence is absent, defendants have objected on evidentiary grounds that the admission of negative or inconclusive scientific evidence is either irrelevant, or alternatively, unfairly prejudicial. This type of objection forces the court to consider the *CSI* Infection head-on because the heightened juror expectation is part of the state's proffer regarding the material relevance and necessity of the evidence for which it is seeking admission. . . .

Although courts have been reluctant to affirmatively rule on the existence of the *CSI* Effect, they are mindful of its potential deleterious impact if left unchecked, and have ruled on evidentiary challenges to allow prosecutors to present this type of evidence. For this reason, courts have found negative scientific evidence to be relevant under the evidentiary requirements for admissibility. Prosecutors want to explain the total story of the crime scene as well as its investigations, including unsuccessful, unavailable, and inclusive test results. It is now common for prosecutors to call a latent fingerprint examiner to testify, even in cases where no fingerprint evidence was found, to explain to the jury why fingerprint evidence is absent from the case. . . .

Distortion of the Meaning of the Evidence

The *CSI* Infection goes well beyond the application of a lower or higher burden of proof; it delves into the realm of warping, skewing, and manipulating the realities of evidence in a way that threatens the accuracy of the verdict and the legitimacy of the criminal justice system. . . .

The danger that the CSI *Infection presents is not that jurors expect more forensic science, but rather that fictional entertainment will lead to misinformation about criminal investigations, prosecutions, and forensic science.*

Multiple factors explain why jurors want more proof. The extreme and recent popularity of fictional crime dramas and forensic crime shows, designed to entertain, is merely one of several important factors. Other factors that may affect jurors' expectations include: (1) the Innocence Project's uncovering of many cases where juror errors, forensic science errors, or eyewitness identification errors resulted in unconscionable stories of innocent men spending decades in jail for crimes they did not commit; (2) the materialization of DNA as a new reliable forensic technology with the remarkable ability to implicate or exonerate the criminally accused; (3) the emergence of the technology era in which science and technology can do more, and do it faster and more accurately than ever before; and (4) the fall from grace of law enforcement due to numerous scandals that exposed corrupt practices such as planting evidence or lying under oath. These factors may encourage citizens to become skeptical of police testimony and the alleged incriminating physical evidence or confessions obtained during a criminal investigation.

As a general proposition, it is important that jurors rigidly hold the government's case to its requisite high burden of proof beyond a reasonable doubt. It is appropriate and reasonable for modern criminal jurors to expect better proof as investigatory technology and forensic techniques improve; however, the danger that the *CSI* Infection presents is not that jurors expect more forensic science, but rather that fictional entertainment will lead to misinformation about criminal investigations, prosecutions, and forensic science. The problem is not merely a television show. The greatest threat is the inappropriate application of fictional analysis in real life cases, which in some instances has induced erroneous conclusions of fact and faulty verdicts. . . .

The crime novels, television shows, and films depicting crimes, criminal investigations, and criminal prosecutions are altered purposely for entertainment purposes, causing the line between reality and fiction to be intentionally blurred by artists to make the film, novel, or television show seem real, yet still entertaining. The artists' motivation is not malicious; instead, it is mainly commercially driven. Nonetheless, the knowledge learned from such sources may trick viewers into believing they are trained to some degree to interpret the law and science.

As the [Donald E.] Shelton [et al.] study [*A Study of Juror Expectations and Demands Concerning Scientific Evidence: Does the "CSI Effect" Exist?*, 2006] suggests, *CSI* watchers have a higher expectation for forensic science evidence. That statistic alone may seem appropriate and non-prejudicial. However, the [N.J.] Schweitzer & [Michael J.] Saks study [*The CSI Effect: Popular Fiction About Forensic Science Affects the Public's Expectations About Real Forensic Science*, 2007] also found that *CSI* watchers are less likely to believe the forensic science presented to them in court. This statistic suggests that high volume *CSI* watchers substitute their own research and expertise, gained from watching entertainment television, for that of the legally qualified experts testifying in court. . . .

While it is true as a matter of law that it is well within the purview of the jury to decide the weight of the evidence and the credibility of the witnesses, it is improper for jurors to base their determinations on fiction. Therefore, it is in the best interest of the larger society to minimize the potential impact that the fictional justice system scripted in Hollywood has upon the real American criminal justice system demystified in actual courtrooms all across the country. . . .

Although some scholars still debate the existence of the *CSI* Effect, as well as the correct title for it, litigators and judges are dealing with the *CSI* Effect. Rulings are based upon the *CSI* Effect, and the *CSI* Effect, thus, operates in real cases on real juries. This [viewpoint] seeks to bridge the gap between the theoretical debate, the limited and early empirical research, and the practical experience of litigators and trial judges. The examination of recent appellate rulings that address various phases of the criminal trial gives additional context to the ongoing conversation. No matter what it is called, there is a real phenomenon occurring in courtrooms all across the nation at both the state and federal levels. The *CSI* Effect must be controlled to ensure fairness within criminal jury trials. Vigilance toward protecting the constitutional fairness of the American criminal justice system can never be too excessive—the stakes are too high and false outcomes are too devastating.

Expectation of Forensic Evidence Has No Bearing on Jurors' Decisions

Donald E. Shelton

Donald E. Shelton is a felony trial judge in Ann Arbor, Michigan, and is on the faculty at Eastern Michigan University.

Crime and courtroom proceedings have long been fodder for film and television scriptwriters. In recent years, however, the media's use of the courtroom as a vehicle for drama has not only proliferated, it has changed focus. In apparent fascination with our criminal justice process, many of today's courtroom dramas are based on actual cases. *Court TV* offers live gavel-to-gavel coverage of trials over the Internet for $5.95 a month. Now, that's "reality television"!

Reality and fiction have begun to blur with crime magazine television shows such as *48 Hours Mystery, American Justice*, and even, on occasion, *Dateline NBC*. These programs portray actual cases, but only after extensively editing the content and incorporating narration for dramatic effect. Presenting one 35-year-old cold case, for example, *48 Hours Mystery* filmed for months to capture all pretrial hearings as well as the 2-week trial; the program, however, was ultimately edited to a 1-hour episode that suggested the crime remained a "mystery" . . . notwithstanding the jury's guilty verdict.

The next level of distortion of the criminal justice system is the extremely popular "reality-based" crime-fiction television drama. The *Law & Order* franchise, for example, appears on television several nights a week promoting plots "ripped from the headlines." It and other television programs pluck an issue suggested by an actual case and weave a story around it.

Donald E. Shelton, "The 'CSI Effect': Does It Really Exist?" *National Institute of Justice Journal*, March 2008.

The most popular courtroom dramas—whether actual, edited, or purely fictional—focus on the use of new science and technology in solving crimes. *CSI: Crime Scene Investigation* has been called the most popular television show in the world. Not only is *CSI* so popular that it has spawned other versions that dominate the traditional television ratings, it has also prompted similar forensic dramas, such as *Cold Case, Bones,* and *Numbers.* According to one 2006 weekly Nielsen rating:

- 30 million people watched *CSI* on one night.

- 70 million watched at least one of the three *CSI* shows.

- 40 million watched two other forensic dramas, *Without a Trace* and *Cold Case.*

Those ratings translated into this fact: five of the top 10 television programs that week were about scientific evidence in criminal cases. Together, they amassed more than 100 million viewers.

How many of those viewers reported for jury duty the next day?

Claims and Commonly Held Beliefs

Many attorneys, judges, and journalists have claimed that watching television programs like *CSI* has caused jurors to wrongfully acquit guilty defendants when no scientific evidence has been presented. The mass media quickly picked up on these complaints. This so-called effect was promptly dubbed the "*CSI* effect," laying much of the blame on the popular television series and its progeny.

I once heard a juror complain that the prosecution had not done a thorough job because "they didn't even dust the lawn for fingerprints." As one district attorney put it, "Jurors now expect us to have a DNA test for just about every case. They expect us to have the most advanced technology possible, and they expect it to look like it does on television."

But is this really the expectation of today's jurors? And if so, is it the fault of *CSI* and its ilk?

To date, the limited evidence that we have had on this issue has been largely anecdotal, based primarily on prosecutor interviews with jurors after trials. Now, however, we have some findings based on a formal study that two researchers and I recently performed.

Gregg Barak, Ph.D., and Young Kim, Ph.D., criminology professors at Eastern Michigan University, and I surveyed 1,000 jurors prior to their participation in trial processes. The prospective jurors were questioned regarding their expectations and demands for scientific evidence and their television-watching habits, including *CSI* and similar programs. Our goal was to determine if there was any empirical evidence behind the commonly held beliefs that juror expectations for forensic evidence—and their demand for it as a condition for conviction—are linked to watching law-related television shows.

What Programs Do Jurors Watch?

In June, July, and August 2006, a written questionnaire was completed by 1,027 randomly summoned jurors in Ann Arbor, Michigan. The potential jurors, who completed the survey prior to any jury selection, were assured that their responses were anonymous and unrelated to their possible selection as a juror.

First, we obtained demographic information and asked the prospective jurors about their television-viewing habits, including the programs they watched, how often, and how "real" they thought the programs were. Then, we tried to determine what these potential jurors expected to see in terms of evidence from the prosecutor.

The survey asked questions about seven types of cases:

1. Every criminal case.

2. Murder or attempted murder.

3. Physical assault of any kind.

4. Rape or other criminal sexual conduct.

5. Breaking and entering.

6. Any theft case.

7. Any crime involving a gun.

With respect to each of these categories of crimes, we then asked what types of evidence the prospective jurors expected to see:

- Eyewitness testimony from the alleged victim.

- Eyewitness testimony from at least one other witness.

- Circumstantial evidence.

- Scientific evidence of some kind.

- DNA evidence.

- Fingerprint evidence.

- Ballistics or other firearms laboratory evidence.

Then, we got to the heart of the matter: not only did we want to explore jury expectations regarding scientific evidence, we also wanted to discover whether the prospective jurors would demand to see scientific evidence before they would find a defendant guilty.

---

46 percent [of jurors surveyed] expected to see some kind of scientific evidence in every criminal case.

We asked the survey participants how likely they would be to find a defendant guilty or not guilty based on certain types of evidence presented by the prosecution and the defense. Using the same cases and evidence described above, we gave potential jurors 13 scenarios and five choices for each:

1. I would find the defendant guilty.

2. I would probably find the defendant guilty.

3. I am not sure what I would do.

4. I would probably find the defendant not guilty.

5. I would find the defendant not guilty.

To help ensure that all of the survey respondents were operating from the same legal guidelines, we gave them the burden of proof and reasonable doubt instructions that are given to all seated jurors in criminal cases in Michigan.

Juror Expectations for Forensic Evidence

Did the survey respondents expect the prosecution to present some kind of scientific evidence? Our survey indicated that:

- 46 percent expected to see some kind of scientific evidence in *every* criminal case.

- 22 percent expected to see DNA evidence in *every* criminal case.

- 36 percent expected to see fingerprint evidence in *every* criminal case.

- 32 percent expected to see ballistic or other firearms laboratory evidence in *every* criminal case.

The findings also suggested that the jurors' expectations were not just blanket expectations for scientific evidence. Rather, expectations for particular types of scientific evidence seemed to be rational based on the type of case. For example, a higher percentage of respondents expected to see DNA evidence in the more serious violent offenses, such as murder or attempted murder (46 percent) and rape (73 percent), than in other types of crimes. Our findings also indicated that a higher percentage wanted to see fingerprint evidence in breaking and entering cases (71 percent), any theft case (59 percent), and in crimes involving a gun (66 percent).

The Envelope, Please . . .

It was not a surprise that *Law & Order* and *CSI* were the two most frequently watched law-related television programs (45 percent and 42 percent, respectively, of the surveyed jurors). We found that frequent *CSI* viewers also frequently watched other law-related programs, and those who did not watch *CSI* tended not to watch such programs. We also found that *CSI* viewers, in general, were more likely to be female and politically moderate. Respondents with less education tended to watch *CSI* more frequently than those who had more education.

As to how "real" a television program was perceived to be, our results indicated that the more frequently jurors watched a given program, the more accurate they perceived the program to be.

What role, then, did watching *CSI* play in the respondents' expectations and demands for forensic evidence?

Potential jurors' increased expectations of scientific evidence did not *translate into a demand for this type of evidence as a prerequisite for finding someone guilty.*

Forensic Evidence and Jury Verdicts

For all categories of evidence—both scientific and nonscientific—*CSI* viewers (those who watch *CSI* on occasion, often, or regularly) generally had higher expectations than non-*CSI* viewers (those who never or almost never watch the program). But, it is possible that the *CSI* viewers may have been better informed jurors than the non-*CSI* viewers. The *CSI* viewers had higher expectations about scientific evidence that was more likely to be relevant to a particular crime than did the non-*CSI* viewers. The *CSI* viewers also had lower expectations about evidence that was less likely to be relevant to a particular crime than did the non-*CSI* viewers.

Although our study revealed that the prospective jurors had high expectations for scientific evidence, the more important question, I believe, is whether those expectations were more likely to result in an acquittal if they were not met. In other words, do jurors *demand* to see scientific evidence before they will find a defendant guilty?

Interestingly, in most of the scenarios presented, potential jurors' increased expectations of scientific evidence did *not* translate into a demand for this type of evidence as a prerequisite for finding someone guilty. Based on our findings, jurors were more likely to find a defendant guilty than not guilty even without scientific evidence *if the victim or other witnesses testified*, except in the case of rape. On the other hand, if the prosecutor relied on circumstantial evidence, the prospective jurors said they would demand some kind of scientific evidence before they would return a guilty verdict.

Our study did not reveal a so-called "CSI effect" at play in courtrooms.

It's Not *CSI!*

There was scant evidence in our survey results that *CSI* viewers were either more or less likely to acquit defendants without scientific evidence. Only 4 of 13 scenarios showed somewhat significant differences between viewers and non-viewers on this issue, and they were inconsistent. Here are some of our findings:

- In the "every crime" scenario, *CSI* viewers were more likely to convict without scientific evidence if eyewitness testimony was available.

- In rape cases, *CSI* viewers were less likely to convict if DNA evidence was not presented.

- In both the breaking-and-entering and theft scenarios, *CSI* viewers were more likely to convict if there was victim or other testimony, but no fingerprint evidence.

Although *CSI* viewers had higher expectations for scientific evidence than non-*CSI* viewers, these expectations had little, if any, bearing on the respondents' propensity to convict. This, we believe, is an important finding and seemingly very good news for our Nation's criminal justice system: that is, differences in expectations about evidence did *not* translate into important differences in the willingness to convict.

That said, we believe it is crucial for judges and lawyers to understand juror expectations for forensic evidence. Even though our study did not reveal a so-called "*CSI* effect" at play in courtrooms, my fellow researchers and I believe that a broader "tech effect" exists that influences juror expectations and demands.

During the past 30 years, scientific advances and discoveries have led to a technology revolution. The development and miniaturization of computers and the application of computer technology to almost every human endeavor have been primary forces in new scientific discoveries. At the same time, new technology has created a revolution in information availability and transmission. The Internet is an obvious example, and, in many ways, it has been the catalyst for this ongoing revolution.

Science and information feed off each other; advancements in science are fostered by the ability of scientists to exchange and transfer information. At the same time, scientific developments almost immediately become available not only to scientists but also to the entire world. It is hardly unexpected that the media grab scientific discoveries and quickly make them part of our popular culture.

Many laypeople know—or think they know—more about science and technology from what they have learned through the media than from what they learned in school. It is those people who sit on juries. Every week, the ever-evolving scientific and information age comes marching through the courtroom door in the psyche of almost every juror who takes a seat in the box.

The Jury Is Always 'Right'

Our legal system demands proof beyond a reasonable doubt before the government is allowed to punish an alleged criminal. When a scientific test is available that would produce evidence of guilt or innocence—but the prosecution chooses not to perform that test and present its results to the jury—it may be reasonable for a jury to doubt the strength of the government's case. This reality may seem unreasonable to some, but that is not the issue. Rather, it is how the criminal justice system will respond to juror expectations.

One response to this change in expectations would be to get the evidence that jurors seek. This would take a major commitment to increasing law enforcement resources and would require equipping police and other investigating agencies with the most up-to-date forensic science equipment. In addition, significant improvements would need to be made in the capacity of our Nation's crime laboratories to reduce evidence backlogs and keep pace with increased demands for forensic analyses.

Another response would be to equip officers of the court (i.e., judges, prosecutors, and defense lawyers) with more effective ways to address juror expectations. When scientific evidence is not relevant, prosecutors must find more convincing ways to explain the lack of relevance to jurors. Most importantly, prosecutors, defense lawyers, and judges should understand, anticipate, and address the fact that jurors enter the courtroom with a lot of information about the criminal justice system and the availability of scientific evidence.

The bottom line is this: Our criminal justice system must find ways to adapt to the increased expectations of those whom we ask to cast votes of "guilty" or "not guilty."

The *CSI* Effect Exists Only in the Minds of Those Who Propose It

Kimberlianne Podlas

Kimberlianne Podlas is an assistant professor of Media Law at the University of North Carolina at Greensboro.

Recently, several newspaper and magazine articles have warned that a "*CSI* Effect" is impacting our criminal justice system. According to these reports, the television drama *CSI: Crime Scene Investigation* is seducing jurors with promises of forensic evidence, thereby causing an epidemic of unjustified acquittals.

Notwithstanding the popularity of such claims, they are not grounded in case-studies or statistical data of increases in acquittals. Rather, they are based on anecdotes about cases wherein law enforcement lost their case while believing it should have won. However, anecdotes are not an adequate substitute for empirical evidence or a logical theory of media influence.

Though research shows that some televised depictions of law enforcement can influence people's beliefs about the legal system, not every depiction does so. Moreover, even where one does, its effect is limited by how viewers interpret its dominant message. Consequently, since *CSI's* narrative focuses on police catching bad guys and celebrates forensics as infallible, it is not clear whether *CSI* helps or harm prosecutors. . . .

Contrary to the hype, the empirical data does not support the existence of a *CSI* Effect—at least not one that perverts guilty verdicts into wrongful acquittals. Indeed, the data shows

Kimberlianne Podlas, "The 'CSI Effect' and Other Forensic Fictions," *Loyola of Los Angeles Entertainment Law Review*, vol. 27, 2007, pp. 87–88, 90–97, 105–106, 120–23, 125. Copyright © 2009 Loyola Law School. All rights reserved. Reproduced by permission.

that *CSI*-viewing mock jurors did not rely on *CSI* factors in reaching their verdicts (to any greater degree than did their non-viewing counterparts). In fact, only a very small portion of either group referenced such factors at all. Accordingly, it does not appear that there is a *CSI* Effect in light of the empirical data. . . .

The *CSI* Effect is premised on the juxtaposition of television's presentation of forensic investigation and its reality. Even though forensic evidence is prevalent on *CSI*, it is a factor in only a small portion of real-life cases. Additionally, many of the techniques shown on *CSI* do not exist. Moreover, [as was reported in the *Washington Post*,] forensic scientists complain of "the perception of near infallibility of forensic science after watching a few episodes of *CSI*."

Proponents of a *CSI* Effect believe that the show instills in its viewers unreasonable expectations about the commonality of forensic evidence and teaches them that proof of guilt is just a simple forensic test away. Thus, when viewers weaned-on *CSI* become jurors, they will expect the prosecution to present forensic evidence as a prerequisite to conviction. If a prosecutor does not supply such evidence—even if it is irrelevant or supplanted by testimonial evidence—jurors will equate its absence with reasonable doubt and they will wrongfully acquit. According to a Peoria prosecutor, presenting less evidence than viewers see on TV "is viewed as reasonable doubt." Furthermore, besides requiring forensic corroboration, *CSI* might cause jurors to demand that such proof exhibit a certain degree of sophistication. Where the prosecution presents forensic evidence that does not resemble *CSI*'s standard, jurors might discount it. This may also [journalist Martha Graybow has written,] "mak[e] it tough for the government to prove cases."

Some believe that this elevates juror expectations to beyond the already-high burden of proof, thereby leading to acquittals. If jurors require forensic evidence to convict—regardless of the strength of testimonial evidence or relevance of forensics the prosecution's burden may rise from proof "beyond a reasonable doubt" to "beyond all doubt." One prosecutor claimed, "We're hearing stories where people, jurors will come back and say: 'There was no DNA test. I expected that. And without that I'm not convinced.'"

It appears that the CSI *Effect better resembles an urban legend among prosecutors and police officers that has gained credence through repetition.*

Importantly, the *CSI* Effect asserts neither that the absence of forensic evidence might tip the scales in an otherwise close case, nor that when forensic evidence is introduced at trial, jurors might scrutinize it more closely than in the past. Though *CSI* might exact these side-effects, the effect law enforcement complains of and that dominates the media, is that in the face of overwhelming proof of guilt, jurors will wrongly acquit.

Evidence of the *CSI* Effect

Despite the magazine covers and newsprint pages warning of a *CSI* Effect, there is "not a shred of evidence" to back it up [according to Simon Cole and Rachel Dioso in the *Wall Street Journal*]. Rather, it appears that the *CSI* Effect better resembles an urban legend among prosecutors and police officers that has gained credence through repetition.

To date, the only proof of a *CSI* Effect is that some individuals believe in one. The study commonly cited to support the effect is a survey by an Arizona prosecutor of other Arizona prosecutors revealing that a majority of Arizona prosecutors believe in a *CSI* Effect. To buttress this perception, prosecutors have pointed to the acquittal of [actor] Robert Blake as evidence of the *CSI* Effect in action. This acquittal, however, may not reflect a miscarriage of justice à la *CSI* Effect, but legitimate doubts about the evidence or weaknesses in the prosecution's case. . . .

Even prosecutors who claim to have experienced the *CSI* Effect firsthand apply the concept to classic reasonable doubt cases, rather than to those boasting overwhelming evidence of guilt. Many cases involve eyewitness testimony, itself known to be questionable, or traditional *physical* evidence (e.g., a murder weapon, bullets or shell casings, proceeds from the crime, a mask or jacket worn by the perpetrator, a car used to flee the scene, or a marked bill used to purchase drugs) as opposed to forensic evidence (that discovered through or subjected to scientific tests). . . .

Accumulating evidence also casts doubt on the *CSI* Effect. Several experts have called the *CSI* effect illusory or incompatible with existing research. First, if *CSI* causes wrongful acquittals, then acquittal rates should have increased (or conviction rates should have decreased). To the contrary, they have not. Statistics from California, Texas, Illinois, and New York show that juries in felony cases convict virtually the same proportion of defendants as they did ten years ago (before *CSI* aired). This is true for crimes that are forensic evidence-intensive (such as rapes and murders) as well as those that are not (such as thefts). . . .

Explaining Perceptions of the *CSI* Effect

Although these anecdotes do not prove a *CSI* Effect, they elucidate reasons that members of law enforcement might believe in one. An advocate's proximity to a case can cause her to overestimate its strengths and underestimate its weaknesses. Research has shown that a person's desire to win influences their cognitive model to fit with that desired outcome. Throughout the decision making process, mental models shift toward coherence; that is, the information is mentally constructed to support a single conclusion. This coherence shift polarizes perceptions of the evidence, so that individuals with a slight inclination toward guilt "[a]mplify their perception of the case."

Conversely, evidence weakly probative of guilt will be ignored or even transformed to create a mental model supporting guilt. Indeed, one study showed that when individuals entrusted with assessing the evidentiary strength of cases were confronted with accumulating information against their original conclusion, those individuals did not reassess their conclusions, but manipulated the new information to conform to their original conclusion. Individuals may selectively attend to evidence supporting their existing view and neglect information disputing it, further justifying their pre-existing impressions.

As a result, an advocate often finds his or her position the most compelling one. In fact, research demonstrates that prosecutors tend to overestimate the strength of their cases. Individuals who are highly motivated to resolve crime or provide justice for victim, such as law enforcement, are also more likely to overestimate the probative value of evidence in favor of guilt. Meanwhile, they attempt to maintain the "illusion of objectivity" or believe that they are being objective. Additionally, prosecutors are privy to information that will never be known by the jury. This information may contribute to the prosecutor's overestimation of the weight of trial evidence. Hence, a prosecutor encountering an acquittal may be mystified when the outcome is not as she expected, and attempt to account for this in some way that maintains her original belief. Attributing an acquittal to a *CSI* Effect is one way of maintaining that belief. It keeps the original assessment of guilt intact and provides an explanation outside of the prosecutor's control. Further, the *CSI* Effect cannot be disproved. (The fact that cases said to evidence the *CSI* Effect exhibit weaknesses that the prosecutors citing them do not see supports this suspicion.)...

How *CSI* May Be Interpreted

Upon watching the program ..., it is not clear that *CSI's* story would produce an anti-prosecution sentiment. Fundamentally, *CSI* is not "about" forensic techniques, rather it is about cops—albeit ones trained in forensics—catching bad guys. Though forensic tests help narrow the field of suspects, the crime is usually solved through the standard tropes of good police work and confessions. Hence, forensics is not the story, but a plot device used to advance the narrative of police solving crimes (and being rather good at it).

Nevertheless, if forensics is read as the dominant narrative, the show celebrates forensics as nearly perfect. The *CSI* Effect presumes that jurors misinterpret the absence of forensic evidence at trial, but *CSI* never takes us into a courtroom—let alone a jury room. Thus, viewers are not taught that the prosecutor must present forensic evidence for the verdict to be guilty (or that when the prosecutor does not do so, the only correct verdict is not guilty). Instead, they are taught that all of the scientific investigation took place long before trial and led to the defendant's arrest. Accordingly, there is no reason to believe that a juror upon noticing the absence of forensic evidence will invert this narrative against the prosecution. It is equally likely that such a juror will interpret *CSI's* dominant narrative (*i.e.*, of perfect forensics identifying the guilty and being the precursor to arrest) to mean that: (1) arrests are based on forensics; (2) forensics proves guilt; and (3) therefore, anyone arrested and on trial has already been proven guilty. This elevates forensics and equates the defendant's status with already-proven actual guilt. Whether viewed through the perspective of cultivation, narrative theory, or common sense, it is difficult to see how this narrative could cultivate anti-prosecution views....

Forty-two assistant district attorneys from the New York area were solicited ... to help identify cases in which they personally had seen a *CSI* Effect....

Nineteen of twenty prosecutors detailed instances where *CSI* had impacted their cases. Yet, a review of the case files confirmed that there was no such impact, at least not a negative one. The disparity between the sincerity of their belief and reality suggests that the *CSI* Effect is a myth that exists in the minds of its acolytes.

The Benefit of *CSI* to Prosecutors

If there is a *CSI* Effect, narrative theory and common sense suggest that it will benefit law enforcement. As noted, *CSI* features the fantastical world of forensics and smart police work. Even the forensic scientists that fear a *CSI* Effect admit that *CSI*'s depictions are of the "'near infallibility of forensic science.'" This story may cultivate the notion that forensic scientists and their methods are legitimate and reliable, thus bolstering the prosecution's case. In addition, jurors who are motivated to punish a wrongdoer can exaggerate the value of scientific evidence, perceiving it as overly conclusive. Indeed, scientific evidence is very seductive to jurors, and they tend to overvalue its probity and overestimate its infallibility.

Fundamentally, CSI *is not "about" forensic techniques, rather it is about cops—albeit ones trained in forensics— catching bad guys.*

Though television portrays police forensics as neutral, legitimate science, it is neither. Forensics is not premised on the objectivity and methodology of science, but on the subjective determinations of law-enforcement-trained technicians. Most crime labs are an arm of law enforcement, staffed by police in lab coats. In fact, the DNA identification technique was developed as a prosecutorial weapon to confirm the identity of a presumed suspect, and not as an investigatory tool, as portrayed on *CSI*. Indeed, the etymology of "forensics" is not the designation of a specialized field of science, such as a physician might specialize in oncology, but a label for the quasi-science practiced by police. . . .

Aside from potential procedural bias, the underlying science of forensics itself is questionable, as some of it barely qualifies as science at all. In fact, many of the "standard" techniques have either never been endorsed by the scientific community or they lack validation studies to support their premises. . . .

What is labeled a CSI *Effect may more accurately be described as a rationalization embraced by members of law enforcement who find themselves on the losing side of a prosecution.*

Even where forensic tests qualify as legitimate "science," entertainment media perpetuates the misguided notion that forensics is immune from mistake. *CSI* features brilliant scientist-cops employing exacting methods and drawing conclusions that are never faulty—at least when it comes to the forensic evidence. Such a portrayal of absolute certainty might lead jurors to overestimate the accuracy of crime scene evidence or to believe it to be more conclusive than it is. . . .

The mock juror deliberation and ADA [assistant district attorneys] survey results do not offer any evidence that a *CSI* Effect is seducing jurors into legally unjustifiable acquittals, but that, like its namesake television show, is merely fiction. If anything, *CSI's* pro-police, pro-forensics story exalts forensics evidence, thereby bolstering it along with the prosecution's case. Consequently, the *CSI* Effect does not warrant criminal justice reforms or increased latitude for prosecutors.

What is labeled a *CSI* Effect may more accurately be described as a rationalization embraced by members of law enforcement who find themselves on the losing side of a prosecution. By attributing a loss to *CSI's* wrongful influence, a prosecutor can obtain an explanation yet maintain a belief that an acquittal was misguided. Although this cognitive rationalization is understandable, it should not be mistaken for empirical proof that the *CSI* Effect operates anywhere other than in the minds of those proposing it.

Wide Media Coverage of the *CSI* Effect May Itself Influence Jury Reactions

Simon A. Cole and Rachel Dioso-Villa

Simon A. Cole is an associate professor of Criminology, Law, and Society at the University of California, Irvine. Rachel Dioso-Villa is a graduate student whom he advises.

Since 2002, popular media has been disseminating serious concerns that the integrity of the criminal trial is being compromised by the effects of television drama. This concern has been dubbed the "*CSI* effect" after the popular franchise *Crime Scene Investigation (CSI)*. Specifically, it was widely alleged that *CSI*, one of the most watched programs on television, was affecting jury deliberations and outcomes. It was claimed that jurors confused the idealized portrayal of the capabilities of forensic science on television with the actual capabilities of forensic science in the contemporary criminal justice system. Accordingly, jurors held inflated expectations concerning the occurrence and probative value of forensic evidence. When forensic evidence failed to reach these expectations, it was suggested, juries acquitted. In short, it was argued that, in cases lacking forensic evidence in which juries would have convicted before the advent of the *CSI* franchise, juries were now acquitting.

The jury is central to American law. The right to a jury trial is "no mere procedural formality, but a fundamental reservation of power in our constitutional structure" [*Blakely v. Washington*]. Although the jury has been much maligned, the

Simon A. Cole and Rachel Dioso-Villa, "Investigating the 'CSI Effect' Effect: Media and Litigation Crisis in Criminal Law," *Stanford Law Review*, vol. 61, April 2009, pp. 1336–41, 1366–73. Copyright © 2009 The Stanford Law Review. All rights reserved. Republished with permission of *Stanford Law Review*, conveyed through Copyright Clearance Center, Inc.

law continues to treat the jury as almost sacred, and many legal scholars and social scientists continue to defend the jury system.

Among the longstanding criticisms of juries has been the claim that juries are subject to media bias. Psychologists have argued that juries can be influenced by pretrial publicity in specific cases, lending support for the need for changes of venue in high profile cases. But, they have also argued that there are more general forms of pretrial publicity, in which media influence may shape jurors' general views about law and crime in ways that affect jury deliberations and verdicts.

The *CSI* effect is supposedly just such a general pretrial publicity effect. It is alleged that media influence causes potential jurors to have distorted views of the capacity—in the broadest sense of that term—of forensic science to generate evidence in criminal prosecutions. These distorted views, it is alleged, actually affect jury verdicts: cases in which jurors would have convicted absent the media influence of *CSI* and similar television programming now result in acquittals or hung juries. As we have argued elsewhere, such charges, if true, would constitute a serious challenge to law's continued faith in the jury and thus raise serious questions about the integrity of the criminal justice system itself.

CSI: Crime Scene Investigation is a primetime American television crime drama. It first appeared on the CBS television network on October 6, 2000. *CSI* is in some sense a standard television crime drama; its innovation is that the protagonists are forensic scientists rather than police detectives, and the plot is driven by the accumulation of forensic evidence rather than the revelation of psychological motive. *CSI* defied conventional wisdom by daring to try to make science "sexy." This turned out to be a stunningly successful innovation, and *CSI* surprised the network by becoming, for a time, the most popular television series in the world. . . .

Wide Media Coverage

The term *CSI* effect appears to have entered the popular lexicon late in 2002 in an article in *Time* magazine. That article described "a growing public expectation that police labs can do everything TV labs can." Even in this early article, the notion of jury taint was present: "This [expectation, forensic scientists] worry, may poison jury pools. . . ." The term appeared a couple of times the following year and more in 2004. In 2005, media coverage of the *CSI* effect exploded. A LexisNexis search found fifty-six newspaper and magazine articles mentioning the *CSI* effect in that year and seventy-eight articles in 2006, the peak year. This coverage included a cover story in *U.S. News & World Report*, as well as coverage in leading science magazines like *National Geographic* and *Scientific American*. Also in 2006, the first full-length book devoted to the *CSI* effect appeared. Media discourse conceptualizes the *CSI* effect as what Professor [Peter] Manning has called a "media loop," a series of back-and-forth interactions between media and what is called, without irony, "reality." The argument is this: Rapid developments and improvements in the power of forensic science inspired media coverage and even fictional television dramas. These media portrayals cause changes in jury behavior in real criminal trials. These changes themselves become the subject of media coverage: media stories about the impact of *CSI* and similar programs on juror behavior. We refer to this last category of media stories as *CSI* effect discourse.

Media coverage shows remarkably little equivocation about the existence of the *CSI* effect. Media reports declare that "[t]here is no debating" the reality of the *CSI* effect, and that "[t]he story lines are fiction. Their effect is real." It is said that "TV is driving jury verdicts all across America," that "TV's False Reality Fools Jurors," and that "*CSI* Has 'Major Effect' On Real Life Juries." An online journal claims that "In many cases across the nation real-life jurors who are fans of *CSI* has

[sic] either caused hung juries or acquitted obviously guilty criminals, claiming the investigators failed to test evidence the way *CSI* does on television." A jury consultant says that "[t]he *CSI* effect is real, and it's profound." The accusations leveled at *CSI* border on charges of jury tampering: one forensic scientist says that *CSI* is "polluting jury pools." The impact of *CSI* is portrayed as irresistible: a prosecutor adds, "Jurors are so influenced by television . . . that it makes it nearly impossible for us. . . ."

[Prosecutors] have claimed that jurors are now holding them to a higher *standard of proof than the traditional 'beyond a reasonable doubt' standard.*

Not only is the media treating the *CSI* effect as a serious problem, but justice system actors are as well. The FBI has produced a video about it. The Maricopa County Attorney (the presiding prosecutor over much of the major metropolitan area surrounding the city of Phoenix, Arizona) has declared that *CSI* has a "real-life impact on justice" and has called on CBS to insert a disclaimer on the program stating that it is fiction. In addition to concerns about the integrity of the jury system, some prosecutors have claimed that the *CSI* effect has altered another pillar of the criminal trial—the standard of proof. They have claimed that jurors are now holding them to a *higher* standard of proof than the traditional "beyond a reasonable doubt" standard. In closing arguments, prosecutors have called this higher standard the "TV expectation." Several legal scholars have noted that, while the notion that forensically-oriented television programs might influence jurors is theoretically plausible, there is, as yet, no convincing evidence of such an effect. Legal scholars have further noted that, from a theoretical point of view, any media influence on juries would be equally likely to have an effect opposite to that most commonly discussed by the media—

that is, forensically-oriented television programming might just as easily make juries more conviction prone as more acquittal prone. Legal scholars have also noted that even if media *influences* jurors, that by no means necessarily translates into changed *verdicts*. They have also noted that no increase in reported jury acquittals has been detected. . . .

View Presented by the Media

A review of media coverage shows that it tends to characterize the *CSI* effect as a well-established phenomenon. For example, based on a content analysis of seventy mass media articles about the *CSI* effect published between 2002 and 2005, [Elizabeth] Harvey and [Linda] Derksen found that the majority of coverage claimed that jurors had formed unrealistic expectations of forensic evidence because of *CSI*. In order to investigate this issue further, we conducted a content analysis of 258 magazine and newspaper articles discussing the *CSI* effect. . . .

We coded the documents for any discussion of the six effects [that *CSI* is said to have on society]. Not surprisingly, many documents mentioned more than one effect. During the coding process we also discovered some new "effects." Only one of these, which we call the "victim's effect," was prevalent enough to add to our coding scheme. The others were not prevalent enough to warrant further discussion. The victim's effect concerns the supposed effect of *CSI* programs on crime victims' behavior. The claim is that victims have increased expectations that law enforcement will collect forensic evidence at a crime scene.

We also coded whether the documents treated the specified *CSI* effect as real or whether they articulated doubt about whether the specified *CSI* effect was actually occurring. Documents were coded for doubt if, for example, they made statements like "[t]he '*CSI* effect' is largely the product of anecdotal evidence." Many documents that were coded for doubt also included statements asserting the reality of the *CSI* effect. . . .

The primary version of the *CSI* effect found in the media is the strong prosecutor's effect of increased juror expectations, which dwarfs all other effects. The rarity of the defendant's effect is also quite striking. In instances where defense attorneys were interviewed, they often mentioned altering their behavior to highlight the lack of forensic evidence at trial (in support of the strong prosecutor's effect), rather than raising the issue that *CSI* has led to jurors viewing government experts and forensic science techniques as having increased credibility. The strong prosecutor's effect appears in the media around seven times as often as the defendant's effect (197 appearances for the strong prosecutor's effect versus 21 for the defendant's effect). If the *CSI* effect is seen as strategic gamesmanship by prosecutors and defenders, our analysis of media content shows that the prosecutors are clearly doing a better job disseminating their message to the media. . . .

In addition, we found that media discussions of the *CSI* effect gave voice to remarkably little skepticism about the claims that the *CSI* effect is actually occurring. For example, of 197 documents mentioning the strong prosecutor's effect, only 34 gave voice to skepticism about the effect actually occurring. This is particularly striking, given that most legal scholars have expressed doubt that *CSI* actually has changed jury behavior. Indeed, several of the 34 articles voicing doubt are profiles of academics, like Donald Shelton or Kimberlianne Podlas, who have done empirical research that casts doubt on the claims advanced on behalf of the strong prosecutor's effect.

In sum, our analysis showed that the media is quite broad in its use of the term "*CSI* effect," using it to convey a wide variety of quite different and sometimes even incompatible ideas, often in the same article. At the same time, it is clear that, by and large, in media discourse, *CSI* effect means the strong prosecutor's effect—an influence on jury behavior in the direction of acquittal. In addition, the media tends to portray the *CSI* effect as an established phenomenon. For example, one article, [by Susan Clairmont,] states, "[i]n an alarming number of cases, jurors found people not guilty of serious violent crimes because they believed police should have presented more, or different, forensic evidence." Media consumers, therefore, are likely to believe that *CSI* is impacting juror behavior, making convictions more difficult to achieve.

A Serious Social Problem?

Aside from the question of whether the *CSI* effect is actually occurring is the question of whether it constitutes a serious social problem. The media discussions of the *CSI* effect are remarkable for their alarmist tone. Media discussions of the litigation explosion invoked "[i]mages of a destructive, elemental force" and described it with terms like "epidemic," "avalanche," "flood," "tidal wave," "deluge," "apocalypse," and "doomsday." Similarly, media discussions of the *CSI* effect use terms like "alarming," "dangerous," and "a big problem," and they suggest that the *CSI* effect "could have serious ramifications for our justice system." This is striking because, as discussed above, empirical evidence supporting this claim is conspicuously lacking. . . .

Jurors who are consumers of the popular media might believe that prosecutors are typically disadvantaged in criminal trials; that high expectations for forensic evidence are "unreasonable"; and that criminal convictions are becoming increasingly rare and difficult to achieve. Jurors who believe these things might be more sympathetic to prosecutors out of sympathy for the perceived underdog or in attempt to correct for the perceived excesses of antecedent juries. Claiming to be *disadvantaged* is a familiar trope in trial advocacy, especially in opening and closing arguments; prosecutors frequently point out that they bear the burden of proof, whereas defense attorneys often refer to their lack of resources or to the awesome power of the state.

As with the litigation explosion, there may be a second-order media effect on juries in criminal law. We might call this the "*CSI* effect effect": juries that have become convinced through media that there is a strong prosecutor's effect that disadvantages prosecutors and has led antecedent juries to acquit inappropriately might tend to sympathize with the prosecution and enact a seemingly "corrective" pro-prosecution bias. But, if there is, in fact, no strong prosecutor's effect, the *CSI* effect effect is essentially an inappropriate pro-prosecution bias. As [Kiara] Okita notes, "the '*CSI* effect' may not be an effect *caused* by the media, but one which has instead been *promulgated* by the media." . . .

> *The* CSI *effect would seem to embody the law's anxiety about the threat to its legitimacy as a truth-producing institution posed by a rival truth-producing institute called "science."*

Ultimately, the strong prosecutor's effect, as easily as it might be—as Harvey and Derksen describe it—"a self-fulfilling prophecy," might just as easily be a self-denying prophecy. By disseminating through the media the notion that the *CSI* effect is occurring, prosecutors may be preventing the strong prosecutor's effect from occurring. And, if the strong prosecutor's effect is *not* occurring, this counteraction may in fact be creating a new effect of its own, *advantaging*, rather than disadvantaging prosecutors. . . .

What cultural values . . . account for the remarkable resonance of the *CSI* effect? To us, the answer seems clear: the rising authority and prestige of science in modern society. Science is popularly associated with such positive values as truth, certainty, goodness, enlightenment, progress, and so on. Law's relationship to science has always been somewhat uneasy. While law has often held high hopes that science would prove effective at resolving disputes without ambiguity, this very potential to be truth-producer is a cause for understandable anxiety on the part of the law. As we have suggested elsewhere, the *CSI* effect would seem to embody the law's anxiety about the threat to its legitimacy as a truth-producing institution posed by a rival truth-producing institute called "science." The discourse among legal actors about the supposed *CSI* effect is rife with lamentations of the law's purported inability to provide proof with the strength that jurors supposedly desire. Whereas the litigation explosion may have resonated with a societal anxiety about relying on law too heavily, the *CSI* effect would seem to resonate with anxieties about using law too little, increasingly abrogating its truth-producing function to science. Whereas the litigation explosion may have articulated fears of hyperlexis [too much law], the *CSI* effect would seem to give voice to fears of what we might call "hyperscientia"—too much science.

CHAPTER 3

Can New Forensic Technologies Determine If Someone Is Lying?

Chapter Preface

The hope of finding a way to tell when someone is lying has existed since the beginning of human history. Various methods have been tried in different cultures. According to legend, in ancient India suspected thieves were placed in a dark room along with a donkey whose tail had been blackened with soot. Told that the donkey would bray if it was touched by a thief, they were instructed to pull its tail, and those that came out with clean hands were considered guilty. This often-cited story does not take into account the possibility that some innocent people might think a donkey would naturally bray when its tail was pulled—which perhaps illustrates the difficulty of devising a test that cannot produce false indications of guilt.

"We've come a long way since the days when donkeys . . . were used to predict when a person was lying," says the blurb for a recent book on professional lie detection techniques. But some experts doubt this. "There is simply no consensus that polygraph evidence is reliable," declared the U.S. Supreme Court in the 1998 case *United States v. Scheffer.* "To this day, the scientific community remains extremely polarized about the reliability of polygraph techniques. . . . There is simply no way to know in a particular case whether a polygraph examiner's conclusion is accurate, because certain doubts and uncertainties plague even the best polygraph exams." It cited scientific studies in which the accuracy rate of the polygraph was determined to be "little better than could be obtained by the toss of a coin."

The polygraph, commonly called a "lie detector," cannot directly determine whether the subject of a test is lying. Rather, it measures the involuntary physiological effects of emotional reactions—increased heart rate, fast breathing, perspiration, and so forth. The theory is that when a person lies, he or she is more emotionally upset than when telling the truth. But innocent people can be nervous throughout the test, and guilty people sometimes try to "beat" it by self-inflicted pain—for example, by putting tacks in their shoes—so that they will feel just as upset when answering one question as another. Thus it has long been known that the results of "lie detector" tests are not reliable, and under most circumstances they are not admissible in court. Their chief forensic value comes from the fact that criminals who expect to be tested are less apt to lie in the first place.

Recently, there have been attempts to devise better technologies for detecting lies, based on analysis not of bodily changes, but of the brain itself, which has been made possible by newly developed methods for observing what is going on in the brain. "Brain fingerprinting®"—a trademarked name for a technique using electroencephalographic (EEG) measurements of brain activity that is being commercially promoted—is one of these; it aims to determine whether someone is concealing knowledge of a crime. It cannot detect lies in general, much less prove guilt; it merely shows a specific brain response when a subject recognizes information that someone not connected with the crime could not know. Another technology is functional Magnetic Resonance Imaging (fMRI) brain scanning, which is widely used for scientific research and medical purposes and is now also being marketed for lie detection. Advocates of these techniques maintain that since thinking involves the brain, there is bound to be some observable indication of what a person is thinking.

Most experts feel that brain scanning has not been sufficiently tested for its results to be used in court. Even if it were admissible, it might be prohibited under the U.S. Constitution's Fifth-Amendment protection against self-incrimination, although in June 2008 a judge in India accepted a brain scan as evidence in a murder trial. Moreover, there is no direct correspondence between brain activity and mental states, since the same parts of the brain are active under different circumstances. Like the polygraph, a brain scan can show only the physical changes associated with a particular state; it cannot detect the state itself.

Neurologist Robert Burton, who in the online magazine *Salon* on September 25, 2007, discussed whether conscious experience can be detected, wrote: "At best, the fMRI is the physiological equivalent of an aerial photograph of a house. It can tell you which rooms are lighted, even the amount of electricity being used in any room, but it cannot tell you what is going on in a lighted room, or even if anyone is home and is aware of the light." Lying is a matter of conscious awareness. If in principle awareness is undetectable, then perhaps a valid means of distinguishing truth from falsehood can never be developed.

Recordings of Brain Activity Show Whether a Fact Is Stored in Someone's Memory

Sam Simon

Sam Simon is an associate editor of Law Enforcement Technology.

The classic police interrogation scene starts with two officers marching into a room. They flop a stack of crime scene photos down in front of a suspect and claim he knows the scene and recognizes the images. But there he sits, stone faced and unshaken, denying any knowledge of the crime. The officers hoped the images would evoke a reaction they could go on, but he gave them nothing. Nothing they could recognize—until now.

A new forensic tool is helping officers access a suspect's mind to determine what information is indeed stored in the brain.

This new innovation, Brain Fingerprinting, is able to determine whether a person has certain information stored in his memory—such as a criminal act. By reading a specific brain response—called a P300 MERMER (Memory and Encoding Related Multi-facet Electronic Response), which the creator of Brain Fingerprinting Dr. Lawrence Farwell discovered—this innovation has played an integral role in freeing an innocent man from jail and securing a confession to an unsolved murder. Implemented in hundreds of other cases, Brain Fingerprinting is emerging as a powerful and highly accurate forensic tool.

Sam Simon, "What You Don't Know Can't Hurt You," *Law Enforcement Technology*, September 2005. Copyright © 2005 Cygnus Business Media. All rights reserved. Reproduced by permission.

The "Ah-ha" Response

DNA, fingerprints and other forms of forensic evidence are currently at the peak of their practice due in part to popular television shows and their ability to help solve crimes. But what may not be as well known is that most evidence of this type is only applicable in an estimated 1 percent of cases. The use of Brain Fingerprinting, however, is estimated to be applicable in 50 and upwards of 75 percent of cases.

Instead of collecting physical artifacts as evidence, Farwell uses a computer to record the brain's activity in response to stimuli presented to the subject.

"There's a particular brain response called a P300 MERMER," explains Farwell, a Harvard graduate and neuroscientist. "A person has this response when they take note of something significant."

The Brain Fingerprinting test is able to determine whether a person has knowledge about a crime or other type of information by recording and comparing the brain's response to three types of visual stimuli: targets, probes and irrelevants. The stimuli consists of words or pictures that are flashed on a computer screen in front of the subject for approximately 3/10 of a second at a time.

The target stimuli provide a control for the testers. Targets are the information crime testers are certain the suspect knows. For example, if a suspect has been told details of a crime and investigators are sure he knows them, those facts could be used as targets. "When the target stimuli is presented, we know the suspect will have a brain response indicating he recognizes it," says Farwell. "The brain will essentially say 'Ah-ha, I recognize that.'" This is the P300 brain pattern that indicates the subject recognizes a word or picture. The subject will have a similar response when presented with other stimuli that is stored in his brain, and these responses can be recognized by a computer.

The irrelevants, as the name implies, have nothing to do with the subject, crime scene or crime. "These are details that could have been relevant details about the crime that are equally plausible for an innocent suspect or a suspect that knows nothing about the crime," explains Farwell, "but they happen not to be correct details." These will have a different response pattern than the targets do.

Mixed in with the targets and irrelevants are probes— items that will be recognizable as salient features of the crime to somebody that was there and knows the details, but not to somebody who is unaware of the specifics of the crime. If the response to a probe stimuli matches the pattern that a target produces, then there is evidence the information of the crime is stored in the testee's brain.

The Brain Fingerprinting test takes the response to target stimuli and uses it as the model for the response a subject's mind will give when presented with stimuli that is stored in the brain. By comparing the response patterns of probes and irrelevants, the test can determine with a high degree of certainty what information is stored in the subject's brain. If the response of the probes are similar to the targets, then the information is present. If it is similar to the irrelevants, the information is not.

"This way we can tell if a person knows the details of the crime that he would have no way of knowing without being there," says Farwell.

Lifting Brain Fingerprints

There are two general applications for which Brain Fingerprinting can be applied. The first concerns testing concealed information regarding events that have already occurred. Dr. Drew Richardson, a 25-year veteran, now retired, of the FBI [Federal Bureau of Investigation] who acted as one of the bureau's top forensic scientists, explains this involves examining suspects of a crime or potential witnesses to see if they have information stored in their brains that would generally not be known by the public, but would be known by somebody who either witnessed or participated in the crime.

The second application is to determine if someone is associated with a group. This capability is what prompted the FBI to aid in funding for the research and development of this technology.

This test does not . . . prove a person's innocence or guilt. It determines whether the person has information about the crime stored in his brain.

Richardson, who acts as vice president for Forensic Operations with Brain Fingerprinting Labs, and Farwell first worked together in the 1990s at the FBI academy. The Brain Fingerprint testing conducted was centered around determining who in a group of people were FBI graduates and who were new agent trainees.

A list of 25 words, acronyms and phrases relating to the graduates instruction or way of life were collected to act as the probes. One of the items used was FD302. To most people this doesn't mean anything. But to an FBI agent, it's the government designation for the piece of paper that is used to record investigative information, subsequently record into file and ultimately testify if it comes to trial. FD302 immediately stands out and rings a bell with an FBI agent, and using this as well as numerous other probes, the test was able to determine with complete accuracy who was an FBI agent.

"If we can do this with the FBI, we can do this with organized crime; the KGB, or its successor SVR [the Russian foreign intelligence service]; and now with terrorist groups, Al Qaeda and so forth," says Richardson.

It's Either There or It Isn't

This test does not, however, prove a person's innocence or guilt. It determines whether the person has information about the crime stored in his brain. Similar to DNA, the sample is given to a scientist, and following a series of tests, it is determined if the samples match. In this case the information stored in the subject's brain either matches the details of the crime or it doesn't.

Brain Fingerprinting also has nothing to do with lie detection. Unlike lie detection, Brain Fingerprinting has been found to be admissible in court. Furthermore, lie detection works on the basis of emotional stress response where Brain Fingerprinting simply measures if a subject knows the details of a crime. Therefore, this test would not work as a general screening tool. It could not be used to test job applicants on various habitual behaviors, drug use, falsification of an application, etc.

There also are certain types of cases where Brain Fingerprinting will not be applicable. Since Brain Fingerprinting detects a record of the crime stored in the brain, investigators need to have a clear idea of the specifics of a crime. The case of a person's disappearance could be a murder or simply a runaway. Not being able to know what crime or any specifics to test for, this test could not be used in such a case.

Brain Fingerprinting ... has nothing to do with lie detection. ... Lie detection works on the basis of emotional stress response where Brain Fingerprinting simply measures if a subject knows the details of a crime.

Similarly in a sexual assault case, everyone may agree on exactly what happened, but they disagree on the intent of the party. Brain Fingerprinting doesn't indicate intent; it only tests whether the subject recalls the unique details of the crime.

Another case where it would not be applicable is if a person already knows every conceivable detail the pre-test investigation can find about the crime. "If somebody has already been convicted, they may know everything about the crime that we can find out, so we can't structure a Brain Fingerprint test," states Farwell. "In order to structure a test, we need probes—the items the individual denies knowing that are specific details about the crime."

The earlier in a case a Brain Fingerprinting test can be applied, the better, says Farwell. "One hour after the crime has been committed, the perpetrator knows everything about the crime and an innocent suspect doesn't know anything about the crime." He adds, once the individual has been arrested or brought in for questioning, he'll know a little bit about the crime, even if he's innocent.

Administering the test before trial also requires less resources since investigators won't have to go through mountains of court documents to figure out what the person does and doesn't know.

Using Brain Fingerprinting early on also can help speed up the investigative process. If there is a group of suspects, the innocent parties will likely be willing to take a Brain Fingerprint test and show they do not have critical knowledge the perpetrator of the crime would have. Detectives are then able to focus the resources of the investigation toward those who are reluctant to take the test or have shown to have knowledge of the crime.

"Although admissible in court, Brain Fingerprinting doesn't have to get to that point," says Farwell. "We can use it to point to the right suspects, illuminate people and rule out individuals as suspects."

What You Know Can Hurt You

In many instances a subject may know details of a crime from news accounts or being interrogated. Those details would not be used as probe stimuli during the Brain Fingerprinting test. "Immediately before the test, we interview the individual and make sure what he's telling us is that these are details about the crime he doesn't know," says Farwell.

To determine what to use as stimuli and what details to question the subject on, an investigation is done before the Brain Fingerprinting test is administered. The investigation determines the salient details about the crime, what to test for (probes) and what the subject knows are the details of the crime (targets).

Even though many murder weapons are items encountered in everyday life, the brain has a unique response depending on the relationship of stored information.

The investigative team will question the subject and ask if he has knowledge about the crime and the details such as the murder weapon, type of car driven, make-up of the crime scene, etc. If he says he doesn't know what the murder weapon was, he would have no idea if it was a bat, knife, gun, etc. During the test, the subject would be instructed that he is going to see the murder weapon flashed on the screen along with other items. "If at this point he doesn't recognize the weapon as being significant in this context, then we have evidence that he in fact does not know what the murder weapon is," says Farwell.

Even though many murder weapons are items encountered in everyday life, the brain has a unique response depending on the relationship of stored information. Farwell explains that things are significant to us in context and it's like a multiple choice test for the brain. A person may use a steak knife every night, he may go hunting with a rifle or shooting with a pistol, but in regards to a crime, only one of these is significant. "If he knows what the murder weapon is, his brain says 'that's it,'" says Farwell. "If the brain doesn't know, it won't respond the same way, and the computer detects which response is received from the individual."

After flashing all stimuli, the computer provides an objective determination of information present or information absent, and a statistical confidence of that determination. "I don't look at a screen and say, 'Oh yeah, I think it looks like he knows it,'" says Farwell. "It doesn't depend on my subjective judgment or someone else's."

Though an information present determination is done objectively, the brainwaves can be produced on a computer screen to show the difference in responses to the target, probe and irrelevant stimuli.

Altered States of Mind

As anyone in law enforcement knows, a majority of crimes are committed while under the influence of a controlled substance. So how does this affect the responses in a Brain Fingerprinting test? Farwell explains people remember very salient activities or events in their lives. Even if someone is a serial killer and only commits a few murders in his life, it's a big event and people tend to remember that.

As a real-life example, JB Grinder was under the influence of drugs and alcohol at the time he murdered Julie Helton. He was also on therapeutic drugs—anti-psychotic medication—at the time of the Brain Fingerprint test, and Farwell notes he got very clear responses from him.

It should be kept in mind a Brain Fingerprinting result is an objective, scientific account of the contents of people's memories. Memory is not perfect, and judges and juries have to take that into account. "If the test returns a positive result—an information present result—then, for whatever reason, the person knows the details about the crime," says Farwell. "These are details the subject would have no reason knowing unless he committed the crime—that's solid evidence."

Any time a negative result is returned in any science, it must be interpreted with caution. The same is true when not getting a match on fingerprints or DNA. It doesn't necessarily prove the person is innocent, it just provides evidence that can be helpful. . . .

Unlike a fingerprint or DNA sample, a criminal's brain is always at the scene, planning, executing and recording the crime.

The Spread of Brain Fingerprinting

Farwell expects Brain Fingerprinting to become universally applied in the law enforcement field, especially early in the investigative process when there are still a number of suspects and an agency wants to know where to direct resources.

Farwell also believes, as happened with DNA, Brain Fingerprinting will spend years getting fully established in the court system. "We're very confident just as Brain Fingerprinting was ruled admissible in the *Harrington* [*v. State of Iowa*] case, it will continue to be ruled admissible," says Farwell. In the Harrington case, there was extensive evidence and expert testimony presented from both for a full day, he says. Provided with the test's record, the judge ruled it was admissible. Even the expert on the other side admitted the science was impeccable. "His words for the science were 'totally perfect' and even I don't say that," says Farwell.

Richardson also sees this technology emerging in a similar manner as other forensic sciences have. "I think that, as with any technique, it will rise or fall on its own merits and should be introduced into court and have the particulars looked at," says Richardson. "I fully believe it is a sound technology and when done properly will meet the various tests that it should properly face."

Unlike a fingerprint or DNA sample, a criminal's brain is always at the scene, planning, executing and recording the crime. Because of this, the technology has the potential to be applicable in an overwhelming number of cases. Now when an officer presents a pile of photos to a suspect, he'll get just the response he is looking for.

Brain Scanning Accurately Detects Lies During Experiments

Malcolm Ritter

Malcolm Ritter is a science writer for the Associated Press.

Picture this: Your boss is threatening to fire you because he thinks you stole company property. He doesn't believe your denials. Your lawyer suggests you deny it one more time—in a brain scanner that will show you're telling the truth.

Wacky? Science fiction? It might happen this summer.

Just the other day I lay flat on my back as a scanner probed the tiniest crevices of my brain and a computer screen asked, "Did you take the watch?"

The lab I was visiting recently reported catching lies with 90% accuracy. And an entrepreneur in Massachusetts is hoping to commercialize the system in the coming months.

"I'd use it tomorrow in virtually every criminal and civil case on my desk" to check up on the truthfulness of clients, said attorney Robert Shapiro, best known for defending O.J. Simpson against murder charges.

Shapiro serves as an adviser to entrepreneur Steven Laken and has a financial interest in Cephos Corp., which Laken founded to commercialize the brain-scanning work being done at the Medical University of South Carolina.

That's where I had my brain-scan interrogation. But this lab isn't alone. Researchers at the University of Pennsylvania have also reported impressive accuracy through brain-scanning

Malcolm Ritter, "Brain Scans as Lie Detectors? A Lying Thief Checks It Out," Associated Press, January 29, 2006. Copyright © 2006 The Associated Press. All rights reserved. Reprinted with permission of the Associated Press.

recently. California entrepreneur Joel T. Huizenga plans to use that work to start offering lie-detecting services in Philadelphia this July.

His outfit, No Lie MRI Inc., will serve government agencies and "anybody that wants to demonstrate that they're telling the truth," he said.

Both labs use brain-scanning technology called functional magnetic resonance imaging, or fMRI. It's a standard tool for studying the brain, but research into using it to detect lies is still in early stages. Nobody really knows yet whether it will prove more accurate than polygraphs, which measure things like blood pressure and breathing rate to look for emotional signals of lying.

But advocates for fMRI say it has the potential to be more accurate, because it zeros in on the source of lying, the brain, rather than using indirect measures. So it may someday provide lawyers with something polygraphs can't: legal evidence of truth-telling that's widely admissible in court. (Courts generally regard polygraph results as unreliable, and either prohibit such evidence or allow it only if both sides in a case agree to let it in.)

Laken said he's aiming to offer the fMRI service for use in situations like libel, slander and fraud where it's one person's word against another, and perhaps in employee screening by government agencies. Attorneys suggest it would be more useful in civil than most criminal cases, he said.

Legal experts and ethicists ... worry about rushing too quickly from the lab to real-world use.

Of course, there's no telling where the general approach might lead. A law review article has discussed the legality of using fMRI to interrogate foreigners in U.S. custody. Maybe police will use it as an interrogation tool, too, or perhaps major companies will find it cheaper than litigation or arbitration when an employee is accused of stealing something important, other observers say.

For his part, Shapiro says he'd switch to fMRI from polygraph for screening certain clients because he figures it would be more reliable and maybe more credible to law enforcement agencies.

In any case, the idea of using fMRI to detect lies has started a buzz among scientists, legal experts and ethicists. Many worry about rushing too quickly from the lab to real-world use. Some caution that it may not work as well in the real world as the early lab results suggest.

And others worry that it might.

Unlike perusing your mail or tapping your phone, this is "looking inside your brain," Hank Greely, a law professor who directs the Stanford Center for Law and the Biosciences, told me a few days before my scan.

Using fMRI data, a computer was able to spot lies in 28 out of 31 volunteers.

It "does seem to me to be a significant change in our ability ... to invade what has been the last untouchable sanctuary, the contents of your own mind," Greely said. "It should make us stop and think to what extent we should allow this to be done."

But Dr. Mark George, the genial neurologist and psychiatrist who let me lie in his scanner and be grilled by his computer, said he doesn't see a privacy problem with the technology.

That's because it's impossible to test people without their consent, he said. Subjects have to cooperate so fully—holding the head still, and reading and responding to the questions, for example—that they have to agree to the scan.

"It really doesn't read your mind if you don't want your mind to be read," he said. "If I were wrongly accused and this were available, I'd want my defense lawyer to help me get this."

So maybe the technology is better termed a "truth confirmer" than lie detector, he said.

Whatever you call it, the technology has produced some eyebrow-raising results. George and his colleagues recently reported that using fMRI data, a computer was able to spot lies in 28 out of 31 volunteers.

I joined an extension of that study. That's why I found myself lying on a narrow table in George's lab while he and his assistants pulled a barrel-shaped framework over my head like a rigid hood. As it brushed the tip of my nose and blotted out the light from the room, I looked straight ahead to see a computer screen, which would be my interrogator.

Then the table eased into the tunnel of the fMRI scanner, a machine the size of a small storage shed. Only my legs stuck out.

As I focused on the questions popping up on the computer screen, the scanner roared like a tractor trying to uproot a tree stump.

It was bombarding me with radio waves and a powerful magnetic field to create detailed images of my brain and detect tiny changes in blood flow in certain areas. Those changes would indicate those areas were working a bit harder than usual, and according to research by George and others, that would in turn indicate I was lying.

Some questions that popped up on that screen were easy: Am I awake, is it 2004, do I like movies. Others were a little more challenging: Have I ever cheated on taxes, or gossiped, or deceived a loved one. As instructed, I answered them all truthfully, pushing the "Yes" button with my thumb or the "No" button with my index finger.

Then, there it was: "Did you remove a watch from the drawer?"

Just a half-hour or so before, in an adjacent room, I'd been told to remove either a watch or a ring from a drawer and slip it into a locker with my briefcase. This was the mock crime that volunteers lied about in George's study. So I took the watch. As I lay in the scanner I remembered seizing its gold metal band and nestling it into the locker.

So, the computer was asking, did I take the watch?

No, I replied with a jab of my finger. I didn't steal nuthin.'

I lied again and again. Other questions about the watch popped up seemingly at random during the interrogation. Is the watch in my locker? Is it in the drawer? Did I steal it from the drawer?

The same questions came up about the ring, and I told the truth about those.

It would be a different computer's job to figure out which I was lying about, the watch or the ring. It would compare the way my brain acted when I responded to those questions vs. what my brain did when I responded truthfully to the other questions. Whichever looked more different from the "truthful" brain activity would be considered the signature of deceit.

Finally, after answering 160 questions over the course of 16 minutes—actually, it was 80 questions two times apiece—I was done. The machine returned me to the bright light of the scanning room.

The computer's verdict? That would take a few days to produce, since it required a lot of data analysis. I didn't mind waiting. It's not like the result would help get me fired, or lose a lawsuit, or send me to jail.

Nobody in George's studies faced consequences like that, which is one reason the lab results may not apply to real-world situations. George has already begun another study in which volunteers face "a little more jeopardy" from the mock crime. He declined to describe it because he didn't want prospective volunteers to hear about it ahead of time. That work is funded by the Department of Defense Polygraph Institute.

Other questions remain. How would this work on people with brain diseases? Or people taking medications? How would this work on people outside the 18-to-50 age range included in George's recent work?

How about experienced liars? George hopes eventually to study volunteers from prisons.

And then there's the matter of the three people who got away with lying in his recent study. For some reason, the computer failed to identify the object they'd stolen. George says he doesn't know what went wrong.

But in a real-world situation, he said, the person being questioned would go through an exercise like the ring-or-watch task as well as being quizzed about the topic at hand. That way, if the computer failed in the experimental task, it would be obvious that it couldn't judge the person's truthfulness.

Because of that, George said, he's comfortable with entrepreneur Laken's plans to introduce the scanning service to lawyers, though just on a limited basis, by the middle of this year. Lab studies are obviously necessary, he said, but "at a certain point you really have to start applying and see how it works. And I think we're getting close."

But Jennifer Vendemia, a University of South Carolina researcher who studies deception and the brain, said she finds Laken's timetable premature. So little research has been done on using fMRI for this purpose that it's too soon to make any judgment about how useful it could be, she said.

Without studies to see how well the technique works in other labs—a standard procedure in the scientific world—its reliability might be an issue, said Dr. Sean Spence of the University of Sheffield in England, who also studies fMRI for detecting deception.

Speaking more generally, ethical and legal experts said they were wary of quickly using fMRI for spotting lies.

"What's really scary is if we start implementing this before we know how accurate it really is," Greely said. "People could be sent to jail, people could be sent to the death penalty, people could lose their jobs."

Greely recently called for pre-marketing approval of lie-detection devices in general, like the federal government carries out for medications.

Judy Illes, director of Stanford's program in neuroethics, also has concerns: Could people, including victims of crimes, be coerced into taking an fMRI test? Could it distinguish accurate memories from muddled ones? Could it detect a person who's being misleading without actually lying?

Her worries multiply if fMRI evidence starts showing up in the courtroom. For one thing, unlike the technical data from a polygraph, it can be used to make brain images that look simple and convincing, belying the complexity of the data behind them, she said.

"You show a jury a picture with a nice red spot, that can have a very strong impact in a very rapid way. . . . We need to understand how juries are going to respond to that information. Will they be open to complex explanations of what the images do and do not mean?"

The procedure is too cumbersome to be used . . . casually.

There's also a philosophical argument in case fMRI works all too well. Greely notes that four Supreme Court justices wrote in 1998 that if polygraphs were reliable enough to use as evidence, they shouldn't be admitted because they would usurp the jury's role of determining the truth. With only four votes, that position doesn't stand as legal precedent, but it's "an interesting straw in the wind" for how fMRI might be received someday, he said.

It didn't take any jury to find the truth in my case.

"We nabbed ya," George said after sending me the results of my scan. "It wasn't a close call."

I was ratted out by the three parts of my brain the technique targets. They'd become more active when I lied about taking the watch than when I truthfully denied taking the ring.

Those areas are involved in juggling the demands of doing several things at once, in thinking about oneself, and in stopping oneself from making a natural response—all things the brain apparently does when it pulls back from blurting the truth and works up a whopper instead, George said.

Of course, nobody is going to make me or anybody else climb into an fMRI scanner every time they want a statement verified. The procedure is too cumbersome to be used so casually, George says.

But he figures that if a perfect lie detector were developed, that practical consideration might not matter. The mere knowledge that one is available, he said, might provoke people to clean up their acts.

"My hope," George said, "would be that it might make the world operate a little bit more openly and honestly."

Hand-Held Lie Detectors May Be Useful for Screening Purposes

Bill Dedman

Bill Dedman is an investigative reporter for MSNBC.com.

The Pentagon will issue hand-held lie detectors this month [April 2008] to U.S. Army soldiers in Afghanistan, pushing to the battlefront a century-old debate over the accuracy of the polygraph.

The Defense Department says the portable device isn't perfect, but is accurate enough to save American lives by screening local police officers, interpreters and allied forces for access to U.S. military bases, and by helping narrow the list of suspects after a roadside bombing. The device has already been tried in Iraq and is expected to be deployed there as well. "We're not promising perfection—we've been very careful in that," said Donald Krapohl, special assistant to the director at the Defense Academy for Credibility Assessment, the midwife for the new device. "What we are promising is that, if it's properly used, it will improve over what they are currently doing."

But the lead author of a national study of the polygraph says that American military men and women will be put at risk by an untested technology. "I don't understand how anybody could think that this is ready for deployment," said statistics professor Stephen E. Fienberg, who headed a 2003 study by the National Academy of Sciences that found insufficient scientific evidence to support using polygraphs for national security. "Sending these instruments into the field in Iraq and

Bill Dedman, "New Anti-Terror Weapon: Hand-Held Lie Detector," *MSNBC*, April 9, 2008. Copyright © 2008 by msnbc.com. Republished with permission of msnbc.com, conveyed through Copyright Clearance Center, Inc.

Afghanistan without serious scientific assessment, and for use by untrained personnel, is a mockery of what we advocated in our report."

The new device, known by the acronym PCASS, for Preliminary Credibility Assessment Screening System, uses a commercial TDS Ranger hand-held personal digital assistant with three wires connected to sensors attached to the hand. An interpreter will ask a series of 20 or so questions in Persian, Arabic or Pashto: "Do you intend to answer my questions truthfully?" "Are the lights on in this room" "Are you a member of the Taliban?" The operator will punch in each answer and, after a delay of a minute or so for processing, the screen will display the results: "Green," if it thinks the person has told the truth, "Red" for deception, and "Yellow" if it can't decide.

The PCASS cannot be used on U.S. personnel, according to a memo authorizing its use, signed in October [2007] by the undersecretary of defense for intelligence, James R. Clapper Jr.

Polygraphs have sparked a fierce debate for at least a century.

The Army has bought 94 of the $7,500 PCASS machines, which are sold by Lafayette Instrument Co. of Lafayette, Ind. The algorithm, or computer program that makes the decisions, was written by the Advanced Physics Lab at Johns Hopkins University. Besides the Army, other branches of the U.S. military have seen the device and may order their own. The total cost of the project so far is about $2.5 million.

Congress has not held any hearings on the PCASS device. Myron Young, a spokesman for the Pentagon's Counterintelligence Field Activity agency, which sponsored development of PCASS, said it informed congressional committees in a memo in November that the device had been approved for use. But five months later, no hearing has been scheduled. Congress has already scaled back its oversight of the polygraph. Five years ago it eliminated a requirement that the Defense Department produce an annual report on polygraph use.

Less Accurate than a Polygraph

Polygraphs have sparked a fierce debate for at least a century. While supporters claim the devices are reliable, the National Academy of Sciences allows only that they're "well above chance, though well below perfection." Polygraphs are not allowed as evidence in most U.S. courts, but they're routinely used in police investigations, and the Defense Department relies heavily on them for security screening.

[The new device] is simple to operate, because judgment of truthfulness is left to the computer.

Both the proponents and critics agree on one thing: This new device is likely to be less accurate than a polygraph, because it gathers less physiological information.

Like a polygraph, the PCASS uses two electrodes to attempt to measure stress through changes in electrical conductivity of the skin. It also gauges cardiovascular activity, though with a pulse oximeter clipped to a fingertip, rather than a polygraph's arm cuff, which has the advantage of measuring both pulse rate and blood pressure. Unlike the polygraph, the PCASS does not measure changes in the rate of breathing, and it has no way to detect countermeasures, or efforts to fool the machine, such as by making unusual movements.

The training is different, too. While polygraph examiners for the Defense Department must have four-year college degrees and experience in law enforcement, the PCASS operators are mostly mid-level enlisted personnel and warrant officers, some as young as 20 years old. While polygraph examiners take a 13-week course and a six-month internship, PCASS operators undergo only one week of training, though most have military training as interrogators. The Defense Department says PCASS is simple to operate, because judgment of truthfulness is left to the computer.

Discarding 'Inconclusives'

The debate over the device's usefulness boils down to a disagreement over its accuracy.

The Pentagon, in a PowerPoint presentation released to msnbc.com through a Freedom of Information Act request, says the PCASS is 82 to 90 percent accurate. Those are the only accuracy numbers that were sent up the chain of command at the Pentagon before the device was approved.

But Pentagon studies obtained by msnbc.com show a more complicated picture: In calculating its accuracy, the scientists conducting the tests discarded the yellow screens, or inconclusive readings.

That practice was criticized in the 2003 National Academy study, which said the "inconclusives" have to be included to measure accuracy. If you take into account the yellow screens, the PCASS accuracy rate in the three Pentagon-funded tests drops to the level of 63 to 79 percent.

Even if you accept the lower accuracy rates, the Pentagon officials say, the device is still better than relying on human intuition.

"Let's take a worst-case scenario here, and let's say PCASS really is 60 percent accurate," said Krapohl, who heads the project for the Defense Academy for Credibility Assessment at Fort Jackson, S.C. "So let's get rid of the PCASS because it makes errors, and go back to the approach we're currently using, which has less accuracy? As you can see, that's really quite untenable if we're interested in saving American lives and serving the interests of our commanders overseas."

Msnbc.com asked Fienberg, a professor of statistics and social sciences at Carnegie Mellon University in Pittsburgh, to review the unclassified Pentagon studies of the PCASS. He said he was not impressed.

"I, like everyone else I know, want the troops in Iraq, in Afghanistan, elsewhere in the world, to be protected," Fienberg said. "I want terrorists to be detected. I do not want to be living in a threatened world, and I want to give my government the best possible advice."

The new device will not be used to make final decisions ... it is intended only to pare down a large group of people to a smaller group that will receive further scrutiny through traditional means.

"They need devices that work. And if they rely on things that really don't work, and act as if they do, we will have a greater disaster on our hands than we already do in the field in Iraq. We simply do not know what a device like this handheld device will produce in that kind of setting, except for the fact that there's scant evidence that it will produce anything of value."

Only 'a Triage Device'

Pentagon officials say that the new device will not be used to make final decisions, that the rules forbid it. They say it is intended only to pare down a large group of people to a smaller group that will receive further scrutiny through traditional means, such as interviews or a full polygraph exam.

"The PCASS is envisioned more or less like a triage device," Krapohl said. "That is, it's not used as a standalone technology to make final decisions regarding a person's truthfulness. . . . There are locals, there are Iraqis and third-country nationals who apply for access to U.S. military bases to provide support functions. And as you might well imagine, there's not really a good way to do a background investigation of these individuals. And so decisions whether to allow them to come on post and to take these jobs are being based on some pretty imprecise methods, primarily interviews and whatever record checks are available. . . . So the idea of adding the PCASS is to incrementally improve the decisions that are made so that we protect our forces."

The term "triage" normally means deciding who gets attention first. But if PCASS is used to pare down a large group to a smaller one, wouldn't a person who's red-lighted be denied access to the military post? Krapohl acknowledges that possibility, saying it's not dissimilar from the ways colleges choose which students to admit.

"Let's say that they have 10 positions that are open, and they have 100 people who apply, which is very realistic," Krapohl said. "Whatever tools you use to make that assessment, 90 people are not going to get that job anyway. So your role as a decision-maker is to help improve your decision process by making sure that those 10 are flawless, that those individuals have nothing in their background to raise your attention. Therefore a commander might be inclined if he tests or she tests 100 people, and you get 50 green lights, . . . to restrict the decisions to just those 50."

The tests before deployment were all conducted on Americans, in English, far from a battlefield.

No harm in that, Krapohl said. "That's how we make decisions for hiring people everywhere, or making decisions on college applications or so forth. Most people are not going to get in. How do you improve the likelihood that those who do get in are going to be good candidates?"

One floor down from Krapohl's office, the lead instructor for the PCASS project, team chief James Waller, said he's confident that the science behind the device is solid.

"Spent 20 years in the military. If I didn't think it would work, I wouldn't put it in the hands of a soldier, 'cause I was a soldier," Waller said. "So it's not perfect, but they don't have a device at all over there to do this kind of work."

Testing Far from a Battlefield

Fueling the debate over the PCASS is the fact that the tests before deployment were all conducted on Americans, in English, far from a battlefield. The Pentagon tested the device on Army recruits at Fort Jackson, S.C., and on civilians in Columbus, Ohio, who answered classified ads. In all, only 226 people were tested in the scientific experiments before the machine was approved for use by soldiers in the field.

"It's virtually impossible to do a validity study in a war zone," Krapohl said.

Lie detectors sometimes work because people believe they work, deterring the wrong people from applying for jobs in the first place, or prompting admissions of guilt during interrogations.

The desire for a portable lie detector at the war front is described in a memo from Camp Cropper, a U.S. Army detention camp on the outskirts of Baghdad. The unclassified memo from April of last year was written by David Thompson, the team leader of the counterintelligence human intelligence support team at Cropper. In screening Iraqis to work as corrections officers and interpreters, Thompson said, the HUMINT collectors (or human intelligence interrogators) are trying to discover who might be involved in militia or insurgent activities, or who might break the rules by passing information from prisoners to people outside the base.

To make these decisions, Thompson wrote, the interrogators often have little more than gut instinct to go on.

"The ability of the collector to filter truth from fiction is highly dependent on the individual collectors training and real world experience," Thompson wrote. "As the demand for HUMINT personnel has risen, the standards we use to select applicants to the HUMINT field has dropped, yielding a higher percentage of young and inexperienced personnel."

So what's needed, Thompson explains, is a machine.

"While not a perfect technological solution that would completely remove the 'human factor,' it appears to be an invaluable tool," Thompson writes. "PCASS is not a system that will remove the need for experienced collectors but rather will enhance their capabilities. . . . If the PCASS system gives a 'red' reading to one of these questions, the collector can focus his efforts on exploitation, and use the traditional skills of a collector to uncover deception or information."

'What's New Here?'

Lie detectors sometimes work because people believe they work, deterring the wrong people from applying for jobs in the first place, or prompting admissions of guilt during interrogations. Thompson explains that may be the most important use of PCASS. "Once this capability is introduced and word spreads of its use, militia or insurgent related individuals will be less likely to attempt to gain admittance" as correctional officers.

Fienberg, the leader of the National Academy of Sciences study, said this memo demonstrates one of his concerns, because the interrogator shifts all of his attention to those who got a red light. The professor said the danger to soldiers doesn't come from the false positive, the person who fails the lie detector test with a red light despite being truthful. Those people just get further scrutiny, or barred from base. The danger, he said, lies in the false negative, the liar who tests "green" and escapes further scrutiny.

"They've been testing polygraph-like devices for a long long time, and this one doesn't look like it works as well as other ones that were discredited," Fienberg said. "I believe we need a different way to think about interrogation and information gathering, instead of using the polygraph as a magic bullet."

The designers of the PCASS said they attempted to make it lean toward detecting deceptive people, because of the disproportionate consequences of green-lighting a liar in a war zone. The Johns Hopkins researchers said they tweaked the algorithm so it takes only a little evidence of deception to turn the lights red. They also tried to minimize the yellow lights, at the Pentagon's request.

But they acknowledged that this was no easy task. They use the word "non-trivial," which in scientific lexicon means a problem is difficult, even unsolvable.

"Determining these decision rules," the researchers wrote, "is both non-trivial and subjective."

Fienberg, the professor of statistics, said the Pentagon's pre-deployment studies have several weaknesses: They're conducted and paid for by the same people promoting the device. They're small studies, involving few people. The mock crime scenarios don't match the stresses of a war. And no allowance was made for differences in language and culture. Finally, they assume that about half the population is telling the truth, and half are lying; in the real world, where the number of liars may be very small, the number of false positives (truthtellers who get a red light) can overwhelm the resources of investigators.

"Ask the question, what's new here?" Fienberg said of the PCASS. "They went to a group that developed a computer-based algorithm that produces green, yellow and red lights. That's the new technology. It's still based on the same noisy psycho-physiological channels for detecting deception. So we have no new way to detect deception. What we've got is a streamlined version of the polygraph. Therefore you would expect this not to be as accurate as the polygraph.

"Almost everything that has gone on since our report was published is obfuscation," Fienberg said, "including the use of the euphemism 'credibility assessment' to describe the DoD [Department of Defense] activities."

Krapohl and the Defense Department say they hope to develop better tools for detecting deception. Meanwhile, by being portable and better than human intuition, PCASS fills a niche in a war zone.

"That's the best that we can do right now," Krapohl said. "But if you come back next year or in five years, I might have a different answer for you."

The PCASS is being developed only for military use. Krapohl said he doesn't foresee it being sold at the pharmacy for use by parents of teenagers, or by the local police.

"I don't want to see a state trooper with one in the back seat asking you what you have in the trunk."

The Assumption That Physical Reactions Can Detect Lying Is Not Valid

Melissa Mitchell

Melissa Mitchell is news editor of the University of Illinois News Bureau.

When a crime has been committed, the usual modus operandi for police detectives and their fictional counterparts has been to dust the scene for fingerprints. And once they have a suspect in custody, out comes the polygraph, or lie detector.

But in today's forensically sophisticated, "CSI"-influenced [television series *CSI: Crime Scene Investigation*] world, polygraphy—which bases its results on functions of the autonomic nervous system—is increasingly dismissed as dated and unreliable. Rapidly replacing older truth-seeking technologies are new brain-based techniques such as functional magnetic resonance imaging (fMRI), and the electroencephalography(EEG)-based technology known as Brain Fingerprinting®.

Because they are "brain-based," both methods have been promoted in the media as being more precise, accurate and trustworthy.

"Functional magnetic resonance imaging and Brain Fingerprinting® have been hailed as the next, best technologies for lie detection in America, particularly in the context of post-9/11 [terrorist attacks of September 11, 2001] anxiety," University of Illinois professor Melissa Littlefield says in an article published in the May issue of the journal *Science, Technology & Human Values.*

"Far from describing the brain and its functions, fMRI and Brain Fingerprinting® produce models of the brain that

Melissa Mitchell, "Scholar Unconvinced New Lie-Detection Methods Better than Old Ones," University of Illinois News Bureau, June 1, 2009. Reproduced by permission.

reinforce social notions of deception, truth and deviance," she concludes in the paper's abstract.

In other words, Littlefield is unconvinced that the new technologies are necessarily superior to the old ones. In fact, the professor of English and of kinesiology and community health believes polygraphy may have more in common with the new technologies than many scientists—particularly neuroscientists—would suggest.

"They would argue that traditional polygraphy tests the autonomic nervous system. That's respiration, heart rate, pulse, electrical skin conductance."

The old and the new deception-detection tools basically rely on the same three assumptions.

But, Littlefield said, using the old-fashioned lie detector, "you're not really getting deception so much as your body's reaction to the stress of deception."

"And they would argue that (with) fMRI, since it's scanning the brain, we're getting closer to the central nervous system, not dealing with the peripheral nervous system. We're dealing with what some say is 'the organ of deceit'—where the lies are happening."

Three Assumptions

But according to Littlefield, the old and the new deception-detection tools basically rely on the same three assumptions.

"The first one is that lies are somehow measurable—that you can see them in the body through increased breathing, heart rate . . . or by looking at the brain." In the latter case, she said, "colloquially, people say 'your brain lights up' in the fMRI scanner."

The second common assumption, she said, is that "when you look at the body and get some kind of information—whether it's pulse rate or blood oxygenation level dependent

(BOLD) signals, or whatever it is that each is measuring—that somehow you're able to see the body in action without needing any interpretation."

Investigators can't actually track people's intentions or behavior by scanning their brains.

The presumption, she said, is that those viewing results of both manners of truth-seeking "somehow see the body in action without needing any interpretation . . . like looking through a window, as opposed to looking at some kind of artistic picture that needs interpretation."

Finally, she said, "they share this assumption that truth and deception are somehow connected. In deception studies, if you're looking at the polygraph or you're looking at the fMRI, the assumption is that truth is the baseline—the factual, the basic, the natural. And to lie is to add a story on top of the truth."

The "good news" in all of this, she said, is that investigators can't actually track people's intentions or behavior by scanning their brains.

"You can't put someone in an fMRI scanner and read their mind or incriminate them, at least in part, because the person would have to lie so still," Littlefield said. "Protocols are such that if you didn't want to have your brain scanned, all you'd have to do is clench your teeth or move your head, and it would create artifacts in the images, and then you can't use them—luckily."

Feeling Safer

Still, she said, those promoting the newer, brain-based deception-detection technologies have had some degree of success in convincing the media and public that new and improved does equal better/safer. And that notion that science and technology can protect us "makes us feel better," she said.

"We want science to be able to answer all our questions somehow—which it can't do. That's the long and the short of it," she said.

The U. of I. [University of Illinois] professor recently finished a yet-to-be-published book, *Tracing Truth: A Cultural History of Deception Detection*. Much of the book is framed by "looking back at the cultural ideologies—those three stories: lies are measurable, the body seems so obvious, and deception and truth are intertwined."

"And I go back to all this media, debate, science fiction and scientific detective fiction from the turn of the 20th century and trace these stories all the way through to current fMRI literatures in the scientific and popular press."

Littlefield is working on another book, tentatively titled *Playing the Role of a Criminalist: Disciplining Narratives in the Forensic Sciences*. Its focus is on "metadisciplinarity."

The book is based, in part, on Littlefield's own interdisciplinary life and career, and examines how a number of disciplines have come together over the past 50 years to become known as the forensic sciences—"whatever that is," she said. The book also explores what Littlefield calls forensic sciences' "interesting relationship with fiction, in particular Sherlock Holmes [detective character in short stories and novels by Sir Arthur Conan Doyle] and 'CSI.'"

"Without these stories, without this literature, I think you'd have a much harder time trying to get the public on board with things like forensics or fMRI or lie detection," she said.

Littlefield recently returned from Denmark, where she designed an fMRI experiment for a project she plans to begin this fall with a team of international, interdisciplinary researchers.

Although Littlefield could not reveal the specifics of the fMRI study, she did say that the researchers plan to investigate the role of the brain's frontal lobes, along with the cognitive process known as executive function (which involves complex decision-making), during various stressful stimuli. She and her team hope to challenge several paradigms that have been taken for granted in both fMRI deception studies and social neuroscience.

In the meantime, Littlefield advises caution when sizing up the promises of those promoting the latest crop of brain-based truth-seeking technologies.

"This 9/11 kind of hype has allowed and fueled this desire both in scientists and the media, and in popular culture, to try to find something to hold onto for security's sake. But I don't think it's really there"—at least not yet, she said.

For now, she added, a more accurate characterization of current developments in deception detection would be to say, "there are *some* scientists who've done particular kinds of studies with a lot of different limitations, and they've found *some* preliminary things about how the brain works."

Brain Scanning Has Not Been Sufficiently Tested for Public Use

Aalok Mehta

Aalok Mehta is a Web journalist for Dana Press, a division of the Dana Foundation that publishes books and ebooks, as well as online content, for readers interested in brain research.

If television is any judge, then neuroscience-based methods of lie detection have already passed the test of public acceptance—even as the feasibility of the technology remains an open question among scientists. A recent episode of *House*, for instance, showed doctors casually outing a deceptive patient while testing for blood vessel anomalies.

This growing disparity between public and scientific understanding of "forensic neuroscience" was one of several pressing issues that brought nearly 200 people to Washington, D.C., Nov. 13–14 [2008] for the first annual meeting of the Neuroethics Society.

Adding to the urgency of the discussion are two recent developments. A pair of companies, Cephos Corp. and No Lie MRI, have gone fully commercial with functional magnetic resonance imaging (fMRI) systems, the most promising brain-scanning method for lie detection, in the past two years— despite objections that the technology is not ready. And in September, an Indian woman was convicted for murder based largely on a widely criticized electroencephalogram, or EEG, test for detecting familiarity with the details of a crime.

Aalok Mehta, "Lie Detection Services Remain Premature, Neuroethicists Say," *Dana Foundation*, January 2, 2009. Copyright © 2009 The Dana Foundation. All rights reserved. Reproduced by permission.

Scientists and philosophers fear that premature use of lie detectors—one of the most advanced of new neuroscience-based technologies with broad social implications—may set a poor precedent.

"I think lie detection is important in and of itself, but it's also important because it's the first of a variety of new neuroscience-based tests that will have potential legal significance: detection of lies, detection of bias, detection of sensation of pain, detection of recognition," Hank Greely, a law professor at Stanford University, said at the meeting.

It's still far too early to tell whether fMRI-based lie detection will become feasible, Greely and other experts said—and that's why the commercial applications are premature and so worrisome.

For example, most fMRI lie-detection studies have been done in controlled lab settings, with homogenous and willing sets of participants, said University of Pennsylvania psychiatry professor Daniel Langleben. The studies usually show average data for an entire group, which don't translate well to testing individuals.

And many of the variables present in real life—such as stress, illness or lack of foreknowledge about what is true and what is false—are often ignored.

Lies could be differentiated from truth in these studies, Langleben said, but only under specific conditions: "We do not know whether it can be actually done in real life. Though there are some reports about it, it has not been published and it has not been independently studied."

Furthermore, when researchers take external factors into account, the data that remain are modest. "When we carefully control for salience (relevance), when we carefully control for every other sensory component of those items, and we carefully control who was studied . . . in the end you are left with very little," Langleben said.

But Steven Laken, president and chief executive officer of Cephos, argued that commercial services provide useful evidence to courts and offer the real-world empirical data needed to answer many outstanding scientific questions.

Ethical Considerations

"The judicial system makes lots of mistakes, and as an ethical society, should we be driving a way to fix a system that's broken?" Laken asked. "Accurate lie detection could help that. It could be a forensic tool. It's not a definite tool, but it could be a forensic tool."

The company has worked hard to put ethics first, he added, including gathering data for three years before going commercial, using independent scientific consultants and fully outlining the limitations and risks of fMRI to potential customers. In the end, Laken added, the reliability of the company's services rival those of many medical tests.

"We've done over 250 scans, and our accuracy rates range from 78 to 97 percent," he said. "We don't need FDA approval for this, but we're getting the kind of data that would be available for submission if it was an equivalent FDA type test."

But fMRI-based lie detection needs to meet a higher standard precisely because of the magnitude of public misconception and the profound consequences of misuse, others countered.

"This is a particularly significant piece of evidence for which we worry not only about reliability but (about) the balance between its probative value and its potential prejudice, and the potential for prejudice here is enormous," Greely said. "There is already some important evidence that jurors . . . tend to take seriously—too seriously—any piece of evidence that comes with neuroscience attached to it."

No one has systematically addressed countermeasures that could fool the system, he added. Studies comparing whether fMRI works better than polygraphy—which detects lies better than chance but has still been deemed inadmissible in many courts—are also lacking.

"I think this is fascinating science," Greely said. "It may have a place in society, it may not. At this point, we don't know, and I think it is reckless and hence unethical for us to proceed to the public use of something so important with so little knowledge about whether it's good or not."

Voice Stress Analysis Cannot Adequately Distinguish Lies from Truth

Kelly R. Damphousse

Kelly R. Damphousse is associate dean of the College of Arts and Sciences and Presidential Professor of Sociology at the University of Oklahoma.

Law enforcement agencies across the country have invested millions of dollars in voice stress analysis (VSA) software programs. One crucial question, however, remains unanswered:

Does VSA actually work?

According to a recent study funded by the National Institute of Justice (NIJ), two of the most popular VSA programs in use by police departments across the country are no better than flipping a coin when it comes to detecting deception regarding recent drug use. The study's findings also noted, however, that the mere presence of a VSA program during an interrogation may deter a respondent from giving a false answer.

VSA manufacturers tout the technology as a way for law enforcers to accurately, cheaply, and efficiently determine whether a person is lying by analyzing changes in their voice patterns. Indeed, according to one manufacturer, more than 1,400 law enforcement agencies in the United States use its product. But few studies have been conducted on the effectiveness of VSA software in general, and until now, none of these tested VSA in the field—that is, in a real-world environment such as a jail. Therefore, to help determine whether VSA is a reliable technology, NIJ funded a field evaluation of two programs: Computer Voice Stress Analyzer® (CVSA®) and Layered Voice Analysis™ (LVA).

Kelly R. Damphousse, "Voice Stress Analysis: Only 15 Percent of Lies about Drug Use Detected in Field Test," *National Institute of Justice Journal*, March 2008, pp. 8–11.

Researchers with the Oklahoma Department of Mental Health and Substance Abuse Services (including this author) used these VSA programs while questioning more than 300 arrestees about their recent drug use. The results of the VSA output—which ostensibly indicated whether the arrestees were lying or telling the truth—were then compared to their urine drug test results. The findings of our study revealed:

- Deceptive respondents. Fifteen percent who said they had not used drugs—but who, according to their urine tests, had—were *correctly* identified by the VSA programs as being deceptive.

- Nondeceptive respondents. Eight and a half percent who were telling the truth—that is, their urine tests were consistent with their statements that they had or had not used drugs—were *incorrectly* classified by the VSA programs as being deceptive.

Using these percentages to determine the overall accuracy rates of the two VSA programs, we found that their ability to accurately detect deception about recent drug use was about 50 percent.

Arrestees who were questioned using the VSA instruments were less likely to lie about illicit drug use compared to arrestees whose responses were recorded by the interviewer with pen and paper.

Based solely on these statistics, it seems reasonable to conclude that these VSA programs were not able to detect deception about drug use, at least to a degree that law enforcement professionals would require—particularly when weighed against the financial investment. We did find, however, that arrestees who were questioned using the VSA instruments were less likely to lie about illicit drug use compared to arrestees whose responses were recorded by the interviewer with pen and paper.

So perhaps the answer to the question "Does VSA work?" is . . . it depends on the definition of "work."

What Is VSA?

VSA software programs are designed to measure changes in voice patterns caused by the stress, or the physical effort, of trying to hide deceptive responses. VSA programs interpret changes in vocal patterns and indicate on a graph whether the subject is being "deceptive" or "truthful."

Most VSA developers and manufacturers do not claim that their devices detect lies; rather, they claim that VSA detects microtremors, which are caused by the stress of trying to conceal or deceive.

VSA proponents often compare the technology to polygraph testing, which attempts to measure changes in respiration, heart rate, and galvanic skin response.

Although some research studies have shown that several features of speech pattern differ under stress, it is unclear whether VSA can detect deception-related stress.

Even advocates of polygraph testing, however, acknowledge its limitations, including that it is inadmissible as evidence in a court of law; requires a large investment of resources; and takes several hours to perform, with the subject connected to a machine. Furthermore, a polygraph cannot test audio or video recordings, or statements made either over a telephone or in a remote setting (that is, away from a formal interrogation room), such as at an airport ticket counter. Such limitations of the polygraph—along with technological advances—prompted the development of VSA software.

Out of the Lab, into the Field

Although some research studies have shown that several features of speech pattern differ under stress, it is unclear whether VSA can detect *deception-related* stress. In those studies that found that this stress *may* be detectable, the deception was relatively minor and no "jeopardy" was involved—that is, the subjects had nothing to lose by lying (or by telling the truth, for that matter). This led some researchers to suggest that if there is no jeopardy, there is no stress—and that if there is no stress, the VSA technology may not have been tested appropriately.

The NIJ-funded study was designed to address these criticisms by testing VSA in a setting where police interviews commonly occur (a jail) and asking arrestees about relevant criminal behavior (drug use) that they would likely hide.

Our research team interviewed a random sample of 319 recent arrestees in the Oklahoma County jail. The interviews were conducted in a relatively private room adjacent to the booking facility with male arrestees who had been in the detention facility for less than 24 hours. During separate testing periods, data were collected using CVSA® and LVA.

The arrestees were asked to respond to questions about marijuana use during the previous 30 days, and cocaine, heroin, methamphetamine, and PCP use within the previous 72 hours. The questions and test formats were approved by officials from CVSA® and LVA. The VSA data were independently interpreted by the research team and by certified examiners from both companies.

Following each interview, the arrestee provided a urine sample that was later tested for the presence of the five drugs. The results of the urinalysis were compared to the responses about recent drug use to determine whether the arrestee was being truthful or deceptive. This determination was then compared to the VSA output results to see whether the VSA gave the same result of truthfulness or deceptiveness.

Can VSA Accurately Detect Deception?

Our findings suggest that these VSA software programs were no better in determining deception about recent drug use among arrestees than flipping a coin. To arrive at this conclusion, we first calculated two percentage rates:

- Sensitivity rate. The percentage of deceptive arrestees correctly identified by the VSA devices as deceptive.

- Specificity rate. The percentage of nondeceptive arrestees correctly classified by the VSA as nondeceptive.

Both VSA programs had a low sensitivity rate, identifying an average of 15 percent of the responses by arrestees who lied (based on the urine test) about recent drug use for all five drugs. LVA correctly identified 21 percent of the deceptive responses as deceptive; CVSA® identified 8 percent.

The specificity rates—the percentage of nondeceptive respondents who, based on their urine tests, were correctly classified as nondeceptive—were much higher, with an average of 91.5-percent accuracy for the five drugs. Again, LVA performed better, correctly identifying 95 percent of the nondeceptive respondents; CVSA® correctly identified 90 percent of the nondeceptive respondents.

We then used a plotting algorithm, comparing the sensitivity and specificity rates, to calculate each VSA program's overall "accuracy rate" in detecting deception about drug use. We found that the average accuracy rate for all five drugs was approximately 50 percent.

Does VSA Deter People from Lying?

Although the two VSA programs we tested had about a 50-percent accuracy rate in determining deception about recent drug use, might their very presence during an interrogation compel a person to be more truthful?

This phenomenon—that people will answer more honestly if they believe that their responses can be tested for accuracy—is called the "bogus pipeline" effect. Previous research has established that it is often present in studies that examine substance use.

To determine whether a bogus pipeline effect existed in our study, we compared the percentage of deceptive answers to data from the Oklahoma City Arrestee Drug Abuse Monitoring (ADAM) study (1998–2004), which was conducted by the same VSA researchers in the same jail using the same protocols. The only differences—apart from the different groups of arrestees—were that the ADAM survey was longer (a 20-minute survey compared with the VSA study's 5-minute survey) and did not involve the use of VSA technology.

In both studies, arrestees were told that they would be asked to submit a urine sample after answering questions about their recent drug use. In the VSA study, arrestees were told that a computer program was being used that would detect deceptive answers.

As VSA programs come under greater scrutiny—due, in part, to reports of false confessions during investigations that used VSA—the overall value of the technology continues to be questioned.

Arrestees in the VSA study were much less deceptive than ADAM arrestees, based on responses and results of the urine test (that is, not considering the VSA data). Only 14 percent of the VSA study arrestees were deceptive about recent drug use compared to 40 percent of the ADAM arrestees. This suggests that the arrestees in the VSA study who thought their interviewers were using a form of "lie detection" (i.e., the VSA technology) were much less likely to be deceptive when reporting recent drug use.

The Bottom Line: To Use or Not Use VSA

It is important to look at both "hard" and "hidden" costs when deciding whether to purchase or maintain a VSA program. The monetary costs are substantial: it can cost up to $20,000 to purchase LVA. The average cost of CVSA® training and equipment is $11,500. Calculating the current investment nationwide—more than 1,400 police departments currently use CVSA®, according to the manufacturer—the total cost is more than $16 million not including the manpower expense to use it.

The hidden costs are, of course, more difficult to quantify. As VSA programs come under greater scrutiny—due, in part, to reports of false confessions during investigations that used VSA—the overall value of the technology continues to be questioned.

Therefore, it is not a simple task to answer the question: Does VSA work? As our findings revealed, the two VSA programs that we tested had approximately a 50-percent accuracy rate in detecting deception about drug use in a field (i.e., jail) environment; however, the mere presence of a VSA program during an interrogation may deter a respondent from answering falsely. Clearly, law enforcement administrators and policymakers should weigh all the factors when deciding to purchase or use VSA technology.

CHAPTER 4

What Improvements in Forensic Technology Are Being Tried?

Chapter Preface

Forensic technologies can be divided into two types: those used for determining what happened at a crime scene, or whether there was in fact any crime at all, and those used to identify suspects. New developments are being made in both of these areas. Technologies of the first type are generally uncontroversial. For example, improved ways of analyzing blood stains can show whether an injury was caused by an attack or an accident; the examination of bones can identify a murder victim long after the event; and new scanning technologies often work better than conventional autopsies for determining the cause of a death. There are no disadvantages to the use of such innovations other than their cost.

Methods of identifying suspects, on the other hand, are rarely adopted without controversy, and almost all of them have both pros and cons. The accuracy rate of these technologies—even those that have been in use for a long time—has not been scientifically determined, except in the case of DNA testing. Police investigators usually feel that an imperfect technology is better than nothing; but many people worry about the false identifications that these technologies can cause. In addition, many are deeply concerned about the privacy issues raised by some of the newer forensic practices.

One such practice is examination of the DNA of a suspect's relatives. When no DNA is available from a suspect to be used for matching with DNA recovered at a crime scene, investigators now sometimes obtain court orders allowing them to use DNA obtained from relatives' past medical tests. If they have no suspect, they even search databases containing the DNA records of convicted criminals and suspects, and scrutinize their relatives when a match with crime scene DNA is found. Some states do not allow lab technicians to give this information to investigators, a policy to which prosecutors strongly object. "It's disgraceful," said William Fitzpatrick, a New York state district attorney, to the *Washington Post*.[1] "If I've got something of scientific value that I can't share because of imaginary privacy concerns, it's crazy. That's how we solve crimes."

Privacy advocates argue that the searching of family DNA records turns relatives into genetic informants without their knowledge or consent. Nevertheless, because a number of violent crimes have been solved in this way, some people see nothing wrong with it. Phyllis Hedge, whose mother-in-law was murdered by a serial killer, said, "Whatever it takes to catch these people who do these atrocities, who have no respect for human life, whatever it takes to get them, is totally appropriate."[2] Others find it extremely disturbing, especially since some local databases include not only convicts and suspects who were not convicted, but victims and even lab employees.

It has been found that crime does tend to run in families—yet of course, in most cases the majority of a criminal's relatives are innocent. Despite efforts to stop the expansion of databases and laws in many states forbidding it, the trend is toward the eventual inclusion of a large percentage of Americans. This means that sooner or later, a great many people not individually suspected of wrongdoing could be under surveillance, a situation that many believe is a violation of the U.S. Constitution's Fourth Amendment ban on unreasonable search and seizure. "The idea of holding people responsible for who they are rather than what they've done could challenge deep American principles of privacy and equality," George Washington University law professor Jeffrey Rosen told the *Washington Post*.[3] "Although the legal issues aren't clear, the moral ones are vexing," he added.

Notes

1. Ellen Nakashima, "From DNA of Family, a Tool to Make Arrests," *Washington Post*, April 21, 2008.
2. Ibid.
3. Ibid.

Improved Techniques for Analyzing Stains Provide Information About Crimes

Matt Martin

Matt Martin is a contributor to the Daily Helmsman, *a newspaper published by University of Memphis students.*

In millionaire Logan Young's house, there was blood everywhere—bloody handprints on the staircase, blood-soaked towels in the kitchen and bathroom and blood on the floor and walls. Young's housekeeper found his body and called police, who initially ruled the death as a "most serious" homicide. Because Young had recently been convicted in a recruitment scandal involving the University of Alabama, police suspected foul play.

But Young's blood told a different story.

When blood pattern expert T. Paulette Sutton analyzed the crime scene, she ruled the death accidental, based on the distribution of the bloodstains in Young's house. Sutton concluded that Young had tripped while walking upstairs, hit his head on the railing and began bleeding badly. Bewildered but conscious, Young began walking through his house, spreading his blood everywhere, drying his head wound on towels in the kitchen and bathroom before passing out. The pattern of bloodstains did not indicate any form of attack had taken place.

Sutton has been solving similar crimes in Memphis [Tenn.] and nationwide for 30 years. Her work includes the identification and analysis of fluid materials at crime scenes.

Sutton was first hired in 1976 as a serologist, or a scientist who identifies body fluids. During her initial work on crime

Matt Martin, "Hot, Nasty, Smelly Work," *Daily Helmsman Online*, April 22, 2009. Copyright © 2010 The Daily Helmsman. All rights reserved. Reproduced by permission.

scenes, she came across some of the first studies on bloodstain pattern analysis—what was then called blood spatter—and said she was "just totally intrigued with what I thought you could learn from it."

The biggest issue in [a crime scene investigator's] work is the number of man-hours required to make sure she has her analyses correct.

"What we're trying to do with the blood pattern analysis," Sutton said, "is determine the physical mechanism by which that bloodstain was created. I'm trying to answer how the blood got there. I'm looking at it from a biological perspective versus a physical phenomenon. I take into consideration the size of the stains and the overall distribution of the pattern. If somebody is hitting someone with a baseball bat, the spatters created are going to be driven away from the victim just like a baseball is being driven away from a baseball bat."

Sutton said at a crime scene, there are "an incredible array of potential stains." "Things that may turn out to be chocolate ice cream, or a spilled soda, or is it blood? What we're doing is looking at what is left over," she said. "We look at the trash. We take these pieces of trash and back-calculate to how this thing happened."

Sutton finds that, just as in the Young case, the biggest issue in her work is the number of man-hours required to make sure she has her analyses correct. "If I go to a scene, it's not going to be unusual that I'm there the better part of the day," she said. "Then I'm looking at the photographs and the videos and the notes for a lot longer after I've left the scene. It takes that long just to collect the raw data."

Hot, Nasty Work

"On television all this work looks glorious," Sutton added, "but it's really just hot, nasty work. It comes complete with smells—man!"

Many crime scene investigators take issue with their work being portrayed as glamorous on television. Television shows such as CBS's *CSI: Crime Scene Investigation*, they say, set unreasonable standards and expectations both in and out of the courtroom. This phenomenon—the influence of *CSI* on the expectations of victims, jurors and even criminals—has been labeled "the *CSI* effect."

Sgt. Connie Justice of the Memphis Police Department said that detectives have to, out of respect for their jobs, be more patient, cautious and considerate than they are portrayed on television.

"The clues have to stack up," Justice said. "Since there's usually not a videotape, it's a 'most likely' situation. There's a novel you can fill up with the time a person was last seen and when their body was recovered. (Detectives) don't want to go out on a limb because there're so many factors that can alter the way someone decays and things like that. Sometimes we get it wrong, I'm sure."

Most new technologies, those that are producing the most accurate analysis of evidence, are concerned with DNA.

Sutton agreed with Justice, saying, "Juries expect all kinds of forensic evidence on every case. That would be great in an ideal world, but sometimes it's just not there. Or sometimes the answer is inconclusive, which they never get on *CSI*. What we say in a courtroom may send an innocent person to jail or turn a guilty person loose. We have to be very judicious about what we're going to say. We've seen instances where juries would acquit an individual because they felt like the state had not done every test that they saw done on *CSI*."

Justice said the *CSI* shows serve a dual purpose.

"They're good in that they get the public interested in what can be done with the upcoming technology," she said, "but they're also bad in that they create too much of an expectation. (Those who watch crime shows) think we can get DNA off of every single object, that there are full staffs analyzing it and that we can get a single answer. If we don't get every type of answer, it's like we've done something wrong. It's a tough act to follow."

Sutton agreed. "It's just so ridiculous," she said. "It's made for television, though. When I sit down to watch a television show, I want to be entertained. (There is a) long litany of things I have to do before I can even make the statement in court that this is blood—that's not very exciting, you would not call that entertainment. So part of it is poetic license, but part of it is just inaccuracies."

Bloodstain pattern analysis is just one of many new technologies forensic analysts are using to solve crimes. Most new technologies, those that are producing the most accurate analysis of evidence, are concerned with DNA.

Justice discussed the innovation of touch DNA, a technology which in 2006 exonerated JonBenét Ramsey's family of her murder. Touch DNA technology examines skin cells left behind at a crime scene. "In the '80s they had to have a quarter of blood," Justice explained. "In the '90s, that standard reduced to the size of a pea. Now, all it takes is a few epithelial (skin) cells. The skin sheds thousands of cells each day, like when you touch a car seat."

But when trying to identify the Ramsey killer, police were stymied by another technology, the CODIS Database.

The CODIS (Combined DNA Index System) Database is a system created by the FBI in 1994 to collect DNA information from criminals. Investigators can compare DNA profiles in the database to material they find on crime scenes in order to identify suspects.

However, CODIS only keeps records of those criminals who have previously been arrested, so only repeat offenders' names come up. Also, much of the time, newly arrested criminals' DNA information isn't put into the CODIS Database, for various reasons. Still, said Lt. Mark Miller of the Memphis Police Department, investigators are using CODIS more diligently in the last several years, and as of 2008, the Database had 6.5 million offender profiles.

Despite the new technologies' exciting and innovative nature, crime shows still do not present them in a realistic light.

Advancement in Identification Methods

Dr. Herbert Leon MacDonell, director of the Laboratory of Forensic Sciences in Corning, N.Y., has been working in crime scene investigation for over 50 years. MacDonell said most new forensic advancements are happening in the field of identification.

"The major changes in forensic science are not the methodology of what we're looking for," MacDonell said, "but how we look for it. The instrumentation has improved considerably. We didn't use to have the scanning electron microscope; we didn't use to have gas chromatography (the ability to separate substances to identify what they're made of). Years ago, we had several good tools, and they were well used. But we did not have DNA."

"The technology you can use to analyze things now is amazing," he added. "You can take a human hair and with neutron activation check the person's diet for the last 10 years."

MacDonell said that, despite the new technologies' exciting and innovative nature, crime shows still do not present them in a realistic light.

"I think our system has been hampered by shows like *CSI*," MacDonell said, "which show people doing things they cannot do, or doing them at a speed that's impossible. I don't care how long you've worked matching bullets, when you have a bullet, you put it in under the microscope, you compare it to the evidence bullet—it's going to take a while. You don't sit down and say, 'Yup, chief, it's a match.' Why don't (the actors) just say, 'We'll drop it off at the lab,' have a commercial, and then it's the next day?"

Special agent and forensic scientist Dan Royce of the Tennessee Bureau of Investigation talked about RUVIS, or the Reflected Ultra-Violet Imaging System, which can detect fingerprints on a crime scene. He also discussed robotic total stations, which are optical surveying devices that scan a crime scene in 360 degrees. "In five minutes," Royce said, "you can have a map of the entire scene."

Royce admitted that new technologies exist alongside traditional ones, and that the new technologies are used mostly when a case is very complicated. "If you have a scene with 80 pieces of evidence," he said, "a total station is more useful than a tape measure."

About the new technologies used on television crime shows, Royce said, "Many of the new technologies are usually used on *CSI* before they're available to real police officers. (Television producers) get their information from scientific journals."

"And a lot of these shows have technology that doesn't exist in reality," he continued. "They do a gas chromatograph, and the suspect's driver's license pops up. That's just not possible."

Nathan Lefebvre, program specialist at the University of Tennessee National Forensic Academy, agreed with Royce, arguing that the main discrepancy between crime scene investigation and *CSI* is time. "We're always increasing efficiency," Lefebvre said, "but we're not at Hollywood efficiency."

Micro-Stamping of Firearms Is Not an Effective Means of Identifying Criminals

Wendy Wang

Wendy Wang is a staff writer for the California Aggie, *the student newspaper of the University of California at Davis.*

UC [University of California] Davis forensic science program researchers testing new microscopic engraving technology on gun firing pins have concluded that while it is feasible, the technology did not work well for all guns and ammunition tested.

"My study shows that while this technology works with some firearms, it also has problems in other firearms," said UC Davis forensic science graduate student Michael Beddow. "At the current time, it is not recommended that a mandate for implementation of this technology in semiautomatic handguns be made. Further testing and analysis is required."

Todd Lizotte of ID Dynamics, located in Londonderry, N.H., developed a way to use an ultraviolet laser to engrave microscopic markings onto firing pins, similar to how codes are engraved onto computer chips.

When the trigger is pulled, the micro-stamped firing pin will hit the primer of the cartridge case and leave the marked code on it. The idea is that the ejected cartridge can be matched to the gun from which it was fired, which is the premise for the Crime Gun Identification Act of 2007.

[California] Governor Arnold Schwarzenegger passed the Assembly Bill 1471 in October 2007, requiring all new models of semiautomatic pistols sold in California after Jan. 1, 2010

Wendy Wang, "Firearms Micro-Stamping Feasible but not Ideal, Experts Say," *California Aggie*, May 23, 2008. Copyright © 2008–2010 California Aggie. Reproduced by permission.

to be engraved with a micro-stamped code in at least two areas of the "internal surface or internal workings parts of a pistol."

Fred Tulleners, director of the Forensic Science Graduate Group, discovered issues with the process.

"When trying new things, we want to really investigate it," he said. "We found it is technologically flawed." Tulleners is the former director of crime labs in the Sacramento and Santa Rosa areas as well as the former director of the California Criminalistics Institute.

Flawed Technology

Beddow tested the micro-stamped firing pins of six different semiautomatic handguns, two semiautomatic rifles and one pump action shot gun at the California Criminalistics Institute and the California Highway Patrol Academy.

Each firing pin contained three different types of codes: an alpha-numerical code on the tip of the firing pin surrounded by a gear code with a bar code going down the length of the firing pin. Recruits fired 2,500 rounds of ammunition to test the durability of repeated firing, Beddow said.

> Concerns with the new technology include the cost of implementing codes on all firing pins and how beneficial the technology will be.

The ammunition was labeled in numerical order and shot through various guns. The cases were then collected in order to see potential change in the legibility of the characters. The firing pins themselves were photographed at intervals to determine if there had been any changes.

"We had mixed results. By and large, [in] most cases, the bar codes and gear codes did not succeed in impact. It has to do with how the firing pin operates. Sometimes they do multiple hits," Tulleners said. "For instance, [in] the AK-47 gangs use, the firing pins make multiple hits [to the cartridge]."

Multiple hits from the firing pin will mar imprints to the cartridge, thus nullifying the effectiveness of the micro-stamping. The most successful code was the alpha-numerical code.

"The alpha-numerical code provided the best quality of the numerical codes. The quality of forgeability of the impression ranged from firearm to firearm; every gun shoots differently and functions different so the legibility was different," Beddow said. "Bottom line, the technology is feasible. However, [it] does not function equally."

The study was supervised by David Howitt, a UC Davis chemical engineering and materials science professor, and was completed and informally released a year ago. The study was peer reviewed by six external reviewers, the National Research Council among them. This March, the council came out with the same conclusions in their report: more research would be needed to prove that firearms identification rests on firmer scientific footing.

Other concerns with the new technology include the cost of implementing codes on all firing pins and how beneficial the technology will be. According to Tulleners, there are three types of shootings: crimes of passion, professional hits and assassinations (which are less solvable) and gang shootings.

"This research conceivably affects gangs. However, we routinely link cartridge cases to guns," Tulleners said. "Without DNA, gangs are notorious for passing guns, and just because you link a cartridge does not mean you'll find who did it. Gangs can deface the firing pin or buy a whole bunch of firing pins and replace them."

As for the cost of the firing pins, Tulleners estimated the engraved firing pins would cost $7.87 or $6.72 each, which is a very conservative estimate. "There is no real benefit to society, and the money is better spent on other progressions in society," he said.

DNA Testing Is Now Being Used with Non-Violent Crimes

Dan Morse

Dan Morse is a staff writer for the Washington Post.

While unusual, here is a crime as alleged by Montgomery County [Maryland] police that joins the list of things harder to get away with in the era of DNA evidence:

Man walks into a Starbucks, says he wants to apply for a job. He's given an application and a complimentary cup of coffee. Minutes later, he walks around the counter and threatens a barista with a ballpoint pen. He flees with $204 from the cash register and keys to another barista's 1993 Nissan Maxima, leaving behind the partially consumed cup of coffee.

Dominic J. Wilson is scheduled to stand trial today [September 8, 2008] in the Starbucks case.

"Saliva," said Ray Wickenheiser, director of Montgomery's crime lab, "is a good source of DNA."

DNA testing in the county is expanding from killings and rapes to less violent robberies, burglaries and drug deals. Prosecutors say this will lead to quicker convictions because defendants will cave and plead guilty. Defense lawyers worry that as more DNA samples are pushed through the county's crime lab, it will boost the odds of false matches.

Turning the Gold Standard into Fool's Gold

"It runs the risk of turning the gold standard of evidence into fool's gold," said Stephen Mercer, a Montgomery lawyer who has taken on so many of these cases lately that one of his clients calls him "the DNA Dude."

Dan Morse, "DNA Testing Expands to Lesser Crimes," The *Washington Post*, September 8, 2008. Copyright © 2008 The Washington Post. All rights reserved. Used by permission and protected by the Copyright Laws of the United States. The printing, copying, redistribution, or retransmission of the Material without express written permission is prohibited. www.washingtonpost.com.

To read how detectives describe the Starbucks case in their arrest documents, the case appears to reside in the gold-standard realm. The incident took place in 2002, so long ago that the Starbucks in question, along Washington Street in downtown Rockville, doesn't exist anymore, although there is a new one around the corner.

For years, detectives didn't make an arrest. They did have a seized coffee cup, though, from which they lifted a DNA sample, according to charging documents filed in Montgomery Circuit Court. In 2007, the details of that sample were entered into a statewide database of convicted felons.

Up popped a connection to Wilson, who shortly after the alleged Starbucks job was arrested on assault and battery charges, according to court records. In March [2008], a Montgomery grand jury indicted Wilson on one count of theft, two counts of robbery and one count of "robbery with a dangerous weapon," according to a copy of the indictment.

Montgomery's crime lab has been dogged by backlogs of several hundred DNA cases. It is generally hard to keep labs fully staffed, in part because analysts are in such demand. Wickenheiser, the lab director who took over in March, said additional employees have cut the backlog to about 100 cases. His staff is running validation tests on new countertop robots that can do such things as automatically extract DNA from other cellular components. Wickenheiser hopes the robots will start producing evidence for cases by the spring. Coupled with a new gene-sequencing machine, the robots could increase DNA analysis output by at least 30 percent, he said.

Wickenheiser said he wants to make DNA testing routine for all robberies and residential burglaries in Montgomery within five years. Already, courthouse attorneys are dealing with more DNA cases.

"In the early days, you would see them in rapes and murders," said Paul DeWolfe, the chief public defender in Montgomery, who says DNA evidence now shows up in virtually every type of crime.

As that happens, evidence technicians are swabbing for DNA on such things as gun handles, car interiors, cocaine bags and articles of clothing used in strangulation attempts. The problem, said Mercer, is that although the evidence can show that a suspect was near the evidence, it doesn't necessarily show that the suspect committed a crime.

An article of clothing used in a strangulation could have been touched by the suspect weeks earlier in innocent fashion, he said. Also, surface samples often require DNA lab analysts to sort out the suspect's DNA from other people's, introducing a greater chance of error.

Wickenheiser said he has established a "prioritization policy" with detectives and prosecutors that is expediting the most urgent cases. He said detectives and prosecutors know to seek other evidence tying suspects to crimes. And he said that as DNA testing gets more exacting, it simply makes sense to use it more. His analysts now can pull evidence out of DNA samples weighing 100 picograms, a picogram being one-trillionth of a gram. Such precision, he said, can also exonerate innocent suspects.

One of Montgomery's top prosecutors, Laura Chase, a deputy state's attorney, said defense lawyers have feared challenging DNA evidence before a jury. As DNA evidence moves to less-violent crimes, she said, "I think it will encourage pleas. It always has encouraged pleas, and that will make the system more efficient."

DNA Samples Can Provide Clues to a Crime Suspect's Physical Appearance

Evan Pellegrino

Evan Pellegrino is a journalism student at the University of Arizona who writes for the Arizona Daily Star.

A strand of hair or a piece of skin can help prove someone was at the scene of a crime—but UA [University of Arizona] researchers are moving way beyond that.

The scientists say their research could provide law-enforcement agencies with a physical description of a suspect who is still at large, using DNA samples recovered at a scene.

After looking at the hair, skin and eye color of about 1,000 University of Arizona students, then comparing the readings to the students' genetic makeup, the researchers have been able to find a way to predict what people will look like, in terms of eye, skin and hair color.

"There are cases when a blood or semen sample is left at a crime scene and there are no witnesses," said Murray Brilliant, a University of Arizona professor at the Steele Children's Research Center. "This can help in an investigative way."

Brilliant leads a research team that studies genetic disorders that affect people's skin color, such as albinism.

While studying the genes responsible for skin pigment disorders, the team found that three or four among about 30,000 total genes control much of a person's pigmentation, which influence skin, hair and eye color.

Evan Pellegrino, "UA Team Adds Precision to DNA Forensics," *Arizona Daily Star*, March 3, 2009. Copyright © 1999–2009 AzStarNet, Arizona Daily Star and its wire services and suppliers and may not be republished without permission. All rights reserved. Reproduced by permission.

By analyzing and identifying variations in those genes, the researchers found that looking at someone's DNA sequence could allow them to make accurate predictions about that person's appearance.

In other words, they found that a small change in a few genes could cause someone's hair to be brown or blond, or their eyes to be blue or green.

"We're trying to understand how human beings make pigment," Brilliant said. "And there's a parallel interest in the forensic community."

If a DNA sample is found at a crime scene through hair, semen or saliva, forensic scientists could look at Brilliant's models and make predictions about what the person who left the evidence may look like.

Predicting Physical Features from DNA

With a DNA sample, the team is currently able to predict someone's hair color to about 80 percent accuracy, eye color to about 75 percent accuracy and skin color to about 50 percent accuracy—percentages the researchers say are relatively accurate considering the broad range of color each of those physical attributes has.

To find the closest match, the researchers compared their subjects' features to hundreds of different eye colors and shades and the 11 skin tones on a dermatological scale. They also found precise levels of melanin—the compounds that affect color—in hair.

Although Brilliant said his laboratory is most interested in researching pigment disorders, he predicts his team's work will have strong implications for forensic scientists.

In fact, the five-year, $680,000 study by the UA team was funded by the U.S. Justice Department with those applications in mind.

Brilliant said that although the technology won't provide law enforcement with an exact image of a crime suspect, it could provide a pretty good idea of what the person might look like. It also could help law-enforcement agencies learn more about unidentified missing victims.

One expert who first heard of the technology on Monday [March 2, 2009] said it could be helpful. "If characteristics like hair color, eye color and ancestry are being predicted, then it's a very welcomed aid, assuming that the technology is reliable," said Bruce Anderson, a UA adjunct assistant professor who has taught courses on forensics and works at the Pima County [Ariz.] Office of the Medical Examiner-Forensic Science Center.

Currently, the technology is too vague to be used as evidence, but Brilliant thinks it could be used as an "investigative tool," narrowing a pool of suspects. "It's not 100 percent, but 80 percent is more accurate than an eyewitness," he said.

While DNA analyses of this nature have been used previously by law-enforcement agencies on a limited basis, Brilliant said those analyses had a more limited scope, such as only looking at race. "This is broader," he said, adding that UA students were a perfect pool to find test subjects because of their diversity.

Because the country is a melting pot of ethnicities, it's important to test different types of people, Brilliant said. "This has been studied in the genes of individuals, but this is the first time it's all been put together, looking across different populations independent of race and ethnicity."

Brilliant said many other laboratories around the world are working on similar research, looking at DNA to determine someone's height, body type and especially behavior.

The statistics show a significant association with genes and physical traits, said Robert Valenzuela, a UA student who conducted the statistical analysis in the study for his doctoral dissertation.

"We feel comfortable with the statistical power," he said.

CT Scanning Has Many Advantages over Conventional Autopsies

Douglas Page

Douglas Page is a writer who focuses on forensic science and medicine.

It may be too soon for a television series titled *CSI: Radiology*, but advanced imaging devices like multidetector computed tomography (MDCT) scanners are already accelerating changes in forensic medical science.

MDCT technology is important to forensic investigators because it is fast, non-invasive, can obtain images without destroying the artifact, and can be used when conventional autopsy may not be feasible or where families may forbid conventional autopsy based on religious beliefs.

(Multidetector CT scanners are similar in concept to original single-ring CT devices, except MDCT scanners have between 4 and 64 detector rings.)

The technology even has wheels.

In the first use of mobile MDCT for a mass fatality incident, researchers in England recently found that MDCT can be operational in temporary mortuaries within 20 minutes of arrival.

Depending on the nature of the incident, three different imaging modalities may be required at conventional disaster morgues: fluoroscopy to screen victims prior to autopsy; plain x-ray for bone examination; and dental x-ray units to document dentition. MDCT provides an alternative or replacement for fluoroscopy and plain film x-ray within temporary morgues.

Douglas Page, "The Virtual Autopsy: The Doctor Will Scan You Now," *Forensic Magazine*, August–September 2008. Copyright © 2010. All rights reserved. Reprinted with permission from *Forensic Magazine*.

"Our data suggest that CT may be adequate as the sole imaging investigation within a mass fatality mortuary," said Guy N. Rutty, MD, of the Forensic Pathology Unit, University of Leicester. Rutty's unit is the world leader in the area of mobile MDCT.

15-Minute Photo

Rutty recently used a mobile MDCT scanner in a disaster mortuary established after a five vehicle fatal traffic incident. Five out of six bodies were successfully imaged by MDCT in about 15 minutes per body, compared to subsequent full radiological analysis of about one hour per case.

Rutty's mobile scanner was powered by diesel generators, but can also be plugged into the electrical grid. A truck transported the scanner and imaging suite, which included air conditioning, telecommunications facilities for remote radiology reporting, hard film printing, and CD burners for data storage.

The scanner can examine single body bags or multiple fragment bags all at the same time without the bags being opened.

Usually, in the primary reception stage in a disaster morgue, fluoroscopy is used first to screen bodies and body parts, followed by further fluoroscopy or x-ray during identification, autopsy, or anthropological stages.

"These can be time-consuming, rate-limiting procedures often requiring manual handling of both the bodies and equipment to insure adequate imaging," Rutty said. Rutty demonstrated that a single CT modality can undertake both of these roles in a single stage, generating both soft tissue and bony images in antero-posterior, lateral, axial, and 3D views within a short time period.

The scanner can examine single body bags or multiple fragment bags all at the same time without the bags being opened, which not only shields radiology technicians from disturbing sights, but also tends to maintain evidence continuity.

"Since radiation dose is not relevant for the deceased, scanned images were obtained at the highest possible resolution to achieve the narrowest possible reconstructed slice thickness," Rutty said. High resolution however introduces two potential problems. First, increasing resolution correspondingly increases heat load on the scanner, which can delay imaging while the unit cools. Secondly, high resolution increases the number and size of the image file, which can be an issue if the images are to be transmitted offsite to obtain a remote radiology report.

Radiological findings in this incident followed a newly designed forensic CT reporting form that includes review of the muscular-skeletal system, cranium, facial bones, spine, axial, appendicular skeleton, central nervous system, cardiovascular system, respiratory system, airway, abdomino-pelvic organs, including upper GI tract, foreign bodies, and personal effects. "We identified the location of personal possessions and could even collect data related to articles of clothing, such as shoe tread patterns," Rutty said. "We identified debris both on and in the bodies, which could be of evidentiary value."

Rutty said MDCT correctly identified the potential causes of death in all victims. Fractures were well seen and could be reconstructed in 3D.

"In many cases, CT showed additional information not easily obtained by autopsy, such as stable fractures and non-hemmorrhagic brain injury," he said.

Be All You Can See

A 2007 military study found MDCT can also be used either to facilitate or reduce the need for conventional autopsy when drowning is the suspected cause of death.

"Determining whether a person found dead in the water has actually drowned is imperative in forensic investigation because becoming submerged in water may be a secondary rather than primary event," said Col. Angela D. Levy, MD, of the Department of Radiology, Uniformed Services University of the Health Sciences in Bethesda, Maryland.

In Levy's study, whole-body MDCT was performed immediately prior to routine autopsy in 28 male subjects who died of drowning. The control group was 12 male subjects who died of sudden death from coronary artery disease.

Digital images were evaluated for such indications as the presence of fluid and sediment in the paranasal sinuses and airways, mastoid air cell fluid, frothy fluid in the airways, and pulmonary opacity. Image findings were then compared with findings from autopsy reports and photographs.

The researchers concluded that MDCT finding of frothy airway fluid or high-attenuation airway sediment is highly suggestive of drowning, and that MDCT findings of pan sinus fluid, mastoid cell fluid, subglottic tracheal and bronchial fluid, and ground-glass opacity within the lung are supportive of drowning in the appropriate scenario.

Levy said MDCT may provide support for the diagnosis of drowning when other causes of death have been excluded by a limited autopsy or external examination of the body.

MDCT has also been shown to be effective in localizing gunshot wound tracks and to aid in forensic autopsies of gunshot wound victims.

In addition to the MDCT-drowning paper, Levy has published studies of the utility of MDCT in gunshot wounds and fire deaths, work that has led many medical examiners to consider adding MDCT to their facilities.

"MDCT speeds recovery of projectile and bullet fragments through precise localization of metallic fragments and aids in the detection of occult trauma," Levy said.

Certain areas of neck and deep pelvis are difficult to dissect. MDCT helps guide the forensic pathologist through these areas.

"Also, MDCT is very helpful in the depiction and classification fractures in severe skull trauma," Levy said.

Picture This

MDCT has also been shown to be effective in localizing gunshot wound tracks and to aid in forensic autopsies of gunshot wound victims.

In forensic investigations of death by suspected projectile injury, plotting the projectile's entry and exit locations, path, and associated tissue trauma can be important in determining the cause and manner of death.

The Armed Forces Institute of Pathology has used MDCT as a non-invasive method to enhance forensic investigation in this area.

"MDCT may guide, direct, or limit forensic autopsy in projectile injury cases, thereby eliminating the need for a complete invasive autopsy," said H. Theodore Harcke, MD, of the Institute's Department of Radiologic Pathology.

In a 2007 study, Harcke compared MDCT to full-body digital radiography (DR) in the postmortem evaluation of gunshot wound victims. Thirteen consecutive male victims had full-body DR and MDCT prior to routine autopsy. According to Harcke, DR successfully identified all metallic fragments, but MDCT was superior in its ability to precisely determine location because it provided 3D anatomic localization. In all cases, MDCT more accurately assessed organ injuries and wound tracks.

Picture of Stealth

MDCT is even finding forensic uses outside of forensic medicine. Swiss researchers, for instance, have devised a way to detect smuggled dissolved cocaine using MDCT scanners.

Smuggled dissolved drugs, particularly cocaine, in bottled liquids, is an ongoing problem at international borders. Common fluoroscopy of packages cannot detect contaminated liquids. Smugglers dissolve the drug and hide it in a few bottles of, say, wine, filling the remainder with uncontaminated liquid, making it easier to go undetected since border checks perform only random samples.

"Our screening method can test all bottles rapidly and noninvasively," said Silke Grabherr, MD, of the Institute of Forensic Medicine, University of Lausanne. Grabherr said the technique is suitable for the examination of large cargos or to confirm suspicions without compromising the packaging.

Cocaine is a candidate contraband because it shows x-ray attenuation. Attenuation is the reduction in amplitude and intensity of a signal, such as an x-ray.

"When a carton of wine bottles contains the same wine, the bottles will have more or less the same mean attenuation on cross-sectional images," Grabherr said. "It should be considered suspicious when the attenuation of some bottles differs from the rest."

Grabherr said MDCT is applicable to other sorts of smuggling, such as contraband hidden inside small sculptures and hollowed fruit.

"Using CT and measuring the mean opacity of the content, differences in hidden drugs can be detected without destroying the carrier," she said.

Grabherr isn't necessarily recommending that expensive MDCT units be deployed at all border stations.

"To employ our method, collaboration between police or customs officials and a medical department is necessary," she said. Scanning can be performed at any facility with a CT scanner.

"If a forensic chemistry department must analyze a confiscated shipment suspected of containing dissolved cocaine or other drug, the screening scan can be helpful to get a first overview to sort our suspicious vessels so more expensive quantitative chemical analysis can be performed on selected items," Grabherr said.

Attempts Are Underway to Make Bite Mark Analysis More Scientific

Todd Richmond

Todd Richmond is a writer for the Associated Press.

It has sent innocent men to death row, given defense attorneys fits, and splintered the scientific community.

For a decade now, attorneys and even some forensic experts have ridiculed the use of bite marks to identify criminals as sham science and glorified guesswork.

Now researchers at Marquette University say they have developed a first-of-its kind computer program that can measure bite characteristics. They say their work could lead to a database of bite characteristics that could narrow down suspects and lend more scientific weight to bite-mark testimony.

"The naysayers are saying, 'You can throw all this out. It's junk science. It's voodoo. This is a bunch of boobs that are causing a lot of problems and heartaches for people,'" said team leader Dr. L. Thomas Johnson, a forensic dentist who helped identify victims of the cannibalistic Milwaukee serial killer Jeffrey Dahmer. "It's a valid science if it's done properly."

Skeptics already are taking shots.

"Scientifically illiterate," Dr. Mike Bowers, a deputy medical examiner in Ventura County and a member of the American Board of Forensic Odontology, said of Johnson's work.

Built around the assumption that every person's teeth are unique, forensic dentistry has used bite impressions to identify criminals for 40 years. Bite marks on a young woman helped convict serial killer Ted Bundy of murdering her and another college student.

Todd Richmond, "Scientists Hope Database of Bite Marks Gives Forensics Teeth," Associated Press, May 16, 2008. Copyright © 2010 by The Associated Press. All rights reserved. Reprinted with permission.

But critics say human skin changes and distorts imprints until they are nearly unrecognizable. As a result, courtroom experts end up offering competing opinions.

"If the discipline lends itself to opposing experts, it's not science," said Peter Neufeld, co-director of the Innocence Project, which works to free wrongfully convicted inmates.

Since 2000, at least seven people in five states who were convicted largely on bite-mark identification have been exonerated, according to the Innocence Project.

In Arizona, Ray Krone was found guilty in 1992 of killing a Phoenix bartender based largely on expert testimony that his teeth matched bites on the victim. He was sentenced to death, won a new trial on procedural grounds, was convicted again, and got life. But DNA testing in 2002 proved he wasn't the killer. Krone was freed and won a spot on the ABC reality show "Extreme Makeover" to remake his teeth.

In Mississippi, forensic odontologist Dr. Michael West has come under fire after he testified in two child rape-murders in the 1990s that bite marks positively identified each killer. Kennedy Brewer was sentenced to death in one case, and Levon Brooks got life in prison in the other.

DNA tests later connected a third man to one of the rapes, and investigators say he confessed to both killings. In Brewer's case, a panel of experts concluded that the bites on the victim probably came from insects. Brewer and Brooks were exonerated this year.

Determined to prove that bite analysis can be done scientifically, Johnson and his team won about $110,000 in grants from the Midwest Forensic Resources Center at Iowa State University and collected 419 bite impressions from Wisconsin soldier volunteers.

They built a computer program to catalog characteristics, including tooth widths, missing teeth and spaces between teeth. The program then calculated how frequently—or infrequently—each characteristic appeared.

Johnson hopes to collect more impressions from dental schools across the country to expand the database into something close to law enforcement's DNA databanks. With enough samples, the software could help forensic dentists answer questions in court about how rarely a dental characteristic appears in the U.S. population. That would help exclude or include defendants as perpetrators, Johnson said.

He acknowledged that his software will probably never turn bite-mark analysis into a surefire identifier like DNA and that he would need tens of thousands of samples before his work would stand up in court.

But "this is the first step toward actually providing science for this type of pattern analysis," Johnson said.

Bowers, who often testifies for the defense in criminal cases, said Johnson should instead study how skin changes can distort bite marks.

Dr. David Sweet, a forensic dentist at the University of British Columbia, said he has been working on a database similar to Johnson's for the past decade. He said he has offered Johnson casts and reproductions of the hundreds of bite impressions he is making.

Dr. Robert Barsley, a Louisiana State University dental professor and vice president of the American Academy of Forensic Science, said he, too, would send Johnson hundreds of bite impressions.

"His work could certainly be a benefit," Barsley said. "I don't think it will solve the problem, but it would be a step in the right direction."

Soil Analysis Is Becoming a Powerful Technique for Crime Investigation

Louise Murray

Louise Murray is a British photojournalist who specializes in wildlife and environmental topics. Her features have been published internationally.

A ce fictional sleuth Sherlock Holmes was 30 years ahead of his time when he linked the soil on a pair of shoes to the scene of a crime. And even now, another century later, the science of geoforensics—the use of particles of soil or rock in criminal investigations—is still in its infancy. However, it's about to grow up.

The first recorded use of geoforensics in criminal investigation took place in 1908, when a German forensic scientist, Georg Popp was called in to help investigate the murder of a certain Margarethe Filbert in Bavaria. The police discovered that the prime suspect had three layers of soil on his shoes. The outer contained traces of brick and coal, matching the area around a castle where the murder weapon was found. The middle layer matched soils found next to the body, and the innermost, or oldest, corresponded with soils on the walkway outside the victim's house. The suspect's alibi was quickly discredited because his shoes were telling a very different story.

Six years later, Dr Edmond Locard, a pioneering French criminologist, established one of the basic principles of forensic science—that when two objects come into contact, each leaves a trace of the encounter on the other, whether it's dust, fibres, hair or soil. This trace evidence can yield vital informa-

Louise Murray, "Geoforensics: The Secrets in the Soil," *Geographical*, January 2007. Copyright © 2007 Geographical Magazine. Reproduced by permission.

tion about where a person has been, where they live and work, their diet, gender and, often most important, with whom they've been in contact. And when gathered at the scene of a crime, it can provide information about those involved in its commission.

So far, so CSI [television show *CSI: Crime Scene Investigation*]. But although the use of trace evidence collected from boots, shoes, tyres and the like has a long history, it's only recently that researchers have begun to focus on finding ways to extract the maximum amount of information of one particular form of evidence—dirt.

SoilFit is a new cross-disciplinary initiative coordinated by Dr Lorna Dawson at the Macaulay Institute in Aberdeen [Scotland]. The project is attempting to link, very precisely, soil samples collected at a crime scene or from a suspect with specific geographical locations and the associated vegetation.

Far from being homogeneous brown dirt, soils are extremely complex and variable, even over short distances. Forensic scientists currently use numerous conventional soil-analysis techniques, noting characteristics such as colour and texture, and making microscopic observations (including palynology, the study of living and fossil pollen and spores) and mineralogical measurements. The SoilFit team's job is to integrate these established methods with the very latest chemical and biological identification techniques.

The New DNA

Over the past 20 years, a great deal of forensic research effort has been put into the use of DNA fingerprinting and matching in criminal investigations, to the point where they have become extremely powerful techniques. "This has meant that other evidence types have become the poor relation," says Dawson, "particularly when it comes to innovation and development. SoilFit will contribute to the ever-growing arsenal of hi-tech weapons in the fight against crime. Who knows, soil evidence could become the new DNA."

However, there is still a place for the old DNA in geo-forensic analysis. One way of characterising a specific soil is to create a DNA profile of the microorganisms present within it, whether bacteria or fungi. These profiles are retrievable even after drying of the soil in the lab or after a rainstorm at a crime site.

Plant debris in the soil also retains the signatures of the waxes that were once present on the cuticle of the living plants, allowing scientists to differentiate between, for example, soils from heath and heather moorland, grassland or pine forests. These biochemical markers can persist in the soil for thousands of years, and have been verified by carbon dating and cross matching to pollen profiles.

A combination of these techniques can direct police investigators to areas of, say mixed birch and scots pine woodland with an understorey of heather. Early results have shown that individual gardens can be identified by soil alone, extending the hope that soil evidence could become much more important in so-called volume crimes such as burglary. When these techniques are combined with GIS mapping—where a standard Ordnance Survey Mastermap base, traditional soil archive data and underlying geological maps are integrated—a powerful new database can be assembled to assist police.

It's in murder cases that geoforensics really comes into its own.

Dawson demonstrated a prototype in Aberdeen. "We focus on the unusual aspects of a soil that might allow us to discriminate it from others," she explains. In this case, the mineral horneblende was found in an acid soil sample from a hypothetical criminal's shoe in the Edinburgh area. Geological map layers enable large tracts of land to be eliminated and acid clay-based soils highlighted. Pine resin was also present, indicating that the sample came from an area of coniferous woodland. When these are overlaid on the previous layers, and combined with road and travel time data within the range of the suspect's alibi, a very small search area results.

Dawson admits, however, that there are gaps in the national soil archives. "They were largely developed to support agriculture," she explains. "So they focus on rural areas, which isn't where most crimes are committed." To fill this gap, degree students are being deployed in urban areas around the country to sample soils in parkland, gardens, commons and industrial scrubland. Early results have shown that individual gardens can be identified by soil alone, extending the hope that soil evidence could become much more important in so-called volume crimes such as burglary.

Decomposing Bodies

However, it's in murder cases that geoforensics really comes into its own. Traditionally, searches for missing bodies are carried out with police dogs and huge manpower resources to cover large areas of ground, looking for obvious signs of ground disturbance or trace evidence left behind by criminals. These searches are very expensive—in terms of both labour and time—are often unproductive and can destroy vital evidence. Hence the desire to develop a viable alternative.

Dawson's colleague at the Macaulay, Professor David Miller, is a specialist in landscape reconstruction. He coordinates a 40-strong international research team—Geoforensics and Information Management for crime Investigation (GIMI)—that is developing non-invasive ways of recognising the graves of murder victims or buried artefacts. The team is focusing particularly on geophysical techniques such as magnetometry and resistivity—the measurement of the variation in the Earth's magnetic and electrical fields caused by buried objects. Such techniques will be familiar to viewers of the [British] Channel 4 television programme *Time Team*, but they have rarely been applied to crime scenes.

Conventional remote-sensing technologies such as aerial and satellite photography are also useful in forensic investigation, especially when particular parts of the spectrum can be highlighted or eliminated. For example, infrared light is useful for detecting the heat given off by buried bodies as they decompose.

"Even the most careful murderer would be hard pushed to restore all of the layers of soil after burying his victim," says geophysicist Alastair Ruffell of Queens University, Belfast, a specialist in remote-sensing technology and a collaborative member of the GIMI network. "We can use multi-spectral imaging to highlight areas of soil disturbance where the underlying geology has been brought to the surface."

Another geophysical technique being applied is radar interferometry, an extremely sensitive form of aerial radar that can detect differences of only a centimetre in ground height—enough to reveal sinkage caused by an earlier burial.

One can't help but wonder what Holmes would have thought of it all.

Research on Decomposing Bodies Provides Important Data for Forensics

Mike Osborne

Mike Osborne is a contributor to Voice of America, an international multimedia broadcasting service funded by the U.S. government.

TV dramas that follow detectives as they investigate a crime have long been a staple of American television. But in recent years, these shows have taken a decidedly graphic turn, focusing on the forensic teams that examine the victim's body and look for evidence that can help investigators bring the killers to justice. While autopsies, blood spatter analysis and DNA research apparently make for entertaining television, Mike Osborne discovered that real forensic science is far less glamorous.

It's a beautiful spring day in East Tennessee. The trees are just putting on leaves and every shrub and wildflower is in full bloom. But as you enter one of the most unusual research facilities in the world, even the sweetest smelling blossoms can't mask the stench of rotting flesh.

This is the Anthropological Research Facility at the University of Tennessee in Knoxville, a facility more commonly referred to as The Body Farm.

Graduate students are carefully brushing away leaves and twigs from a patch of ground at the edge of a gravel path. They're looking for the last few small bones of a human skeleton. Clipboard in hand, Kate Driscoll checks off each bone as it's discovered, while Brannon Hulsey places them in a plastic collection bag.

Mike Osborne, "The Body Farm: Unique Forensic Research Facility," *Voice of America*, May 13, 2008.

"At this point we're doing pretty well," Driscoll reports. "We're missing about . . . yeah, about five to ten finger and wrist bones, which is not too bad. Usually you're missing a lot more distal toe phalanges—to the very ends of your toes. They're really small and they get lost very easily."

To find those last few bones, Driscoll and Hulsey use mason's trowels to scrape up a thin layer of topsoil and sift it through a metal screen.

They seem oblivious to the many bodies lying under the trees around them. There are currently more than 160 cadavers interred on the Body Farm, which encompasses just a half-hectare of land. Some are little more than bones, but others are in various stages of decay. It's a gruesome sight but Driscoll says the worst part of her work is the odor. "It's actually not as much as you would expect. But in the height of summer, when you have newly decomposing bodies, it gets pretty stinky," she admits with a laugh. "We're having a good day today."

While working with rotting corpses may not be for everyone, it's a price students like Hulsey and Driscoll are willing to pay for a chance to be involved in cutting edge research.

When it opened in 1981, the Anthropological Research Center was the first facility of its kind in the world, and it is still one of only three such research centers, all in the United States.

Researcher Rebecca Wilson oversees body farm operations, which she says provide extremely important information for law enforcement. "How do we decompose? What do we look like at different stages of decomposition? If I have a body that's been dead for three days, what does that look like and can I tell you it's been dead for three days?"

Graduates of the program have gone on to work with law enforcement agencies around the world, and criminologists come to Tennessee to sharpen their skills. "We work with the National Forensic Academy, as well as the FBI, in training their officers on how to recover remains in an outdoor context; be it on the surface or in a burial environment."

Wilson says the Center also collaborates with law enforcement agencies to research specific crimes. "What we'll do is simulate that scenario—usually a differential decomposition, where something doesn't decompose the way it's expected to," she explains. "Is this natural, or is this because what the perpetrator did? But we will simulate a scenario like that and see if it is related to natural processes, or related to the incident." Just such a project is underway this spring in collaboration with an Australian researcher.

Remarkably, all the remains interred at the body farm are donated.

Of course, these studies wouldn't be possible without a steady supply of bodies. Remarkably, all the remains interred at the body farm are donated. "We started our body donation program in 1981," Wilson says. "That year we received 4 donations. Last year we received 116 donations." She says that could be related to those TV crime dramas. "We've seen a significant increase since 2000, which is the same time that your popular television shows have taken off. We have seen an almost exponential increase."

Wilson says it's a diverse group of individuals who donate their bodies to the Center; everyone from a Circuit Court judge to schoolteachers. Once the decomposition of their remains is studied at the body farm, graduate students like Driscoll and Hulsey collect the bones and place them in a permanent research collection housed at the University of Tennessee.

Rebecca Wilson says bones always have a story to tell. With the University of Tennessee's Forensic Anthropology Department preparing to move into a new, larger facility, it's a story scientists like Wilson will be better able to tell.

Organizations to Contact

The editors have compiled the following list of organizations concerned with the issues debated in this book. The descriptions are derived from materials provided by the organizations. All have publications or information available for interested readers. The list was compiled on the date of publication of the present volume; the information provided here may change. Be aware that many organizations take several weeks or longer to respond to inquiries, so allow as much time as possible.

American Academy of Forensic Sciences (AAFS)
410 N 21st St., Colorado Springs, CO   80904
(719) 636-1100 • fax: (719) 636-1993
Web site: www.aafs.org/yfsf

AAFS is a multi-disciplinary professional organization that provides leadership to advance science and its application to the legal system. The Young Forensic Scientists Forum (YFSF) is a group within the AAFS that is dedicated to the education, enrichment, and development of emerging forensic scientists and future leaders of the field. Its Web site has detailed information about careers in forensic science and links to resources dealing with specific fields of specialization. The AAFS also disseminates information via its *Journal of Forensic Sciences* and newsletters.

American Society of Crime Laboratory Directors (ASCLD)
139K Technology Dr., Garner, NC   27529
(919) 773-2044 • fax: (919) 773-2602
Web site: www.ascld.org

ASCLD is a nonprofit professional society of crime laboratory directors and forensic science managers dedicated to providing excellence in forensic science through leadership and innovation. Its Web site's Visitor Center includes a page for students containing detailed information about careers in forensic science.

Crime Lab Project

11278 Los Alamitos Blvd., Suite 351, Los Alamitos, CA   90720
Web site: www.crimelabproject.com

The Crime Lab Project is a nonprofit organization, started by writers and producers but now including many members of the general public, which works to increase awareness of the problems facing public forensic science agencies. It seeks greater support and resources for crime labs, coroner and medical examiners' offices, and other public agencies using forensic science. Its Web site includes a blog with news of interest to supporters plus several interesting quizzes dealing with current issues in forensics.

Crime Lab Report

1921 W Wilson St., Suite A-252, Batavia, IL   60510
(866) 674-9194 • fax: (866) 809-4301
e-mail: editors@crimelabreport.com
Web site: www.crimelabreport.com

Crime Lab Report is an independent organization that analyzes media coverage, public policy trends, and current issues affecting the profession of forensic science and its stakeholders. Its Web site contains archives of its reports plus links to many forensic science sites.

ExploreForensics

e-mail: info@exploreforensics.co.uk
Web site: www.exploreforensics.co.uk

ExploreForensics is a British Web site formed to offer a reference point for the public on forensic science, crime scene investigations, and pathology. Its aim is to be totally objective and unbiased and it does not accept any advertising. The site contains more than eighty articles written by experts who continually update and add new content.

Forensic Magazine

4 Limbo Lane, Amherst, NH   03031

(603) 672-9997 • fax: (603) 672-3028
Web site: www.forensicmag.com

Forensic Magazine is a bimonthly publication of "resources, products, and services" containing detailed articles on equipment and procedures used in all areas of forensic technology. Complete archives are online at its Web site, which also includes Web-only articles and news of interest to those working in the field.

Innocence Project
100 Fifth Ave., 3rd Floor, New York, NY   10011
(212) 364-5340
e-mail: students@innocenceproject.org
Web site: www.innocenceproject.org

The Innocence Project is a national litigation and public policy organization dedicated to exonerating wrongfully convicted people through DNA testing and reforming the criminal justice system to prevent future injustice. Its Web site contains a detailed listing of cases in which unvalidated or improper forensic science contributed to the wrongful conviction. In addition it includes the stories of people who were wrongfully accused between the ages of fourteen and twenty-two and exonerated years later through DNA testing, with suggestions for creating class presentations and papers about them and becoming active in the effort toward reform.

International Crime Scene Investigators Association (ICSIA)
15774 S LaGrange Rd., Orland Park, IL   60462
(708) 460-8082
Web site: www.icsia.org

ICSIA is an Internet-based organization created to assist law enforcement personnel who are involved in the processing of crime scenes. Although most of its Web site is accessible only to members, it includes a public section offering a detailed job description and many links to other sites dealing with crime scene investigation.

Law Enforcement Technology

11720 Beltsville Dr., Suite 300, Beltsville, MD   20705
Web site: www.officer.com/magazines/let

Law Enforcement Technology is a monthly magazine written for members of law enforcement management but of interest to other readers looking for information. Complete archives from 2005 onward are available at its Web site, and each issue contains one or more informative articles about recent forensic technologies.

National Academy of Sciences (NAS)

500 Fifth St. NW, Washington, DC   20001
Web site: www.nasonline.org

NAS is an honorific society of distinguished scholars engaged in scientific and engineering research, dedicated to the furtherance of science and technology and to their use for the general welfare. Among many other activities, it produced—with National Research Council support—the 2009 report *Strengthening Forensic Science in the United States: A Path Forward*, which is discussed in Chapter One of this book, and the entire text of which is available at www.nap.edu/openbook.php?record_id=12589.

National Institute of Justice (NIJ)

810 Seventh St. NW, Washington, DC   20531
(202) 307-2942 • fax: (202) 307-6256
Web site: www.ojp.usdoj.gov/nij/topics/forensics

NIJ is the research, development, and evaluation agency of the U.S. Department of Justice. Its Office of Investigative and Forensic Sciences works to improve the quality and practice of forensic science through support of research and development, testing and evaluation, information exchange, and the development of training resources for the criminal justice community. Its Web site contains many downloadable publications, such as *Crime Scene Investigation: A Guide for Law Enforcement*, plus archives of its magazine *NIJ Journal*, containing articles on all types of forensic technology.

Truth in Justice

e-mail: truthinjustice@gmail.com
Web site: www.truthinjustice.org

Truth in Justice is a nonprofit organization working to educate the public about the vulnerabilities in the U.S. criminal justice system that make the criminal conviction of wholly innocent persons possible. Its Web site has over 1,600 pages of information and resources dealing with the wrongful conviction of such persons. Its page on "Junk Science in the Courtroom" contains articles on how invalid forensic science leads to convictions, plus news stories about cases where this has happened or where misconduct has existed in crime labs.

U.S. National Library of Medicine (NLM)

8600 Rockville Pike, Bethesda, MD   20894
(888) 346-3656
Web site: www.nlm.nih.gov/visibleproofs

NLM—the world's largest medical library—collects materials and provides information and research services in all areas of biomedicine and health care. Its subsite "Visible Proofs: Forensic Views of the Body" contains an exhibition about the history of forensics and educational material for students and teachers, including online activities and lesson plans that introduce forensic medicine, anthropology, technology, and history. It also offers many links to related sites of interest to high school students.

U.S. Senate Committee on the Judiciary

224 Dirksen Senate Office Bldg., Washington, DC   20510
Web site: http://judiciary.senate.gov

One of the oldest regular standing committees of the U.S. Senate, the U.S. Senate Committee on the Judiciary serves as a forum for the public discussion of social and constitutional issues. The Committee is also responsible for oversight of key activities of the executive branch, and is responsible for the initial stages of the confirmation process of all judicial nominations for the federal judiciary. In 2009, the Committee held a hearing on the current state of forensic science, based on the National Academy of Sciences report that it had commissioned. The text of all the testimony given at the hearing is available on its Web site at http:/judiciary.senate.gov/hearings/hearing.cfm?id=4038.

Bibliography

Books

Ken Adler

The Lie Detectors: The History of an American Obsession. New York: Free Press, 2007.

Jay D. Aronson

Genetic Witness: Science, Law, and Controversy in the Making of DNA Profiling. New Brunswick, NJ: Rutgers, 2007.

Bill Bass and Jon Jefferson

Death's Acre: Inside the Legendary Forensic Lab, the Body Farm Where the Dead Do Tell Tales. New York: Berkley, 2004.

Bill Bass and Jon Jefferson

Beyond the Body Farm: A Legendary Bone Detective Explores Murders, Mysteries, and the Revolution in Forensic Science. New York: Morrow, 2007.

George Clarke

Justice and Science: Trials and Triumphs of DNA Evidence. New Brunswick, NJ: Rutgers, 2008.

Simon A. Cole

Suspect Identities: A History of Fingerprinting and Criminal Identification. Cambridge, MA: Harvard University Press, 2002.

W. Mark Dale and Wendy S. Becker

The Crime Scene: How Forensic Science Works. New York: Kaplan, 2007.

Federal Bureau of Investigation	*FBI Handbook of Crime Scene Forensics.* New York: Skyhorse, 2008.
Jim Fisher	*Forensics Under Fire: Are Bad Science and Dueling Experts Corrupting Criminal Justice?* New Brunswick, NJ: Rutgers, 2008.
Jim Fraser	*Forensic Science: A Very Short Introduction.* New York: Oxford University Press, 2010.
Stuart H. James and Jon J. Nordby, eds.	*Forensic Science: An Introduction to Scientific and Investigative Techniques,* 3rd ed. Boca Raton, FL: CRC Press, 2009.
Stephen A. Koehler	*Jumped, Fell, or Pushed: How Forensics Solved 50 "Perfect" Murders.* Pleasantville, NY: Readers Digest Association, 2009.
Michael Kurland	*Irrefutable Evidence: Adventures in the History of Forensic Science.* Chicago: Ivan R. Dee, 2009.
Henry C. Lee	*Blood Evidence: How DNA Is Revolutionizing the Way We Solve Crimes.* New York: Basic Books, 2003.
Henry C. Lee, Elaine M. Pagliaro, and Katherine Ramsland	*The Real World of a Forensic Scientist: Renowned Experts Reveal What It Takes to Solve Crimes.* Amherst, NY: Prometheus Books, 2009.
D.P. Lyle	*Forensics for Dummies.* Chichester, NH: Wiley, 2004.

D.P. Lyle — *Forensics: A Guide for Writers.* Cincinnati, OH: Writer's Digest Books, 2008.

Michael Lynch, Simon A. Cole, et al. — *Truth Machine: The Contentious History of DNA Fingerprinting.* Chicago: University of Chicago Press, 2009.

Myriam Nafte — *Flesh and Bone: An Introduction to Forensic Anthropology.* Durham, NC: Carolina Academic Press, 2009.

National Research Council — *Strengthening Forensic Science in the United States: A Path Forward.* Washington, DC: National Academies Press, 2009.

Michael Newton — *The Encyclopedia of Crime Scene Investigation.* New York: Facts on File, 2008.

David Owen — *Hidden Evidence: 50 True Crimes and How Forensic Science Helped Solve Them.* Buffalo, NY: Firefly Books, 2009.

Katherine M. Ramsland — *The C.S.I. Effect.* Waterville, ME: Thorndike Press, 2007.

Katherine M. Ramsland — *Beating the Devil's Game: A History of Forensic Science and Criminal Investigation.* New York: Berkley, 2008.

Katherine M. Ramsland — *True Stories of CSI: The Real Crimes Behind the Best Episodes of the Popular TV Show.* New York: Berkley, 2008.

Katherine
M. Ramsland

The Devil's Dozen: How Cutting-Edge Forensics Took Down 12 Notorious Serial Killers. New York: Berkley, 2009.

Linda Volonino
and Reynaldo
Anzaldua

Computer Forensics for Dummies. Indianapolis, IN: Wiley, 2008.

Periodicals

Sharon Begley

"Mind Reading Is Now Possible," *Newsweek*, January 21, 2008.

Stephanie Booth

"I Fight for Wrongly Convicted Prisoners," *Cosmopolitan*, September 2005.

Sean Cavanagh

"Forensics Courses Becoming Classroom Fixture," *Education Week*, October 28, 2009.

Christian Science Monitor

"From Lindbergh to Laci, a Growing Forensics Fancy," April 24, 2003.

Emily Costello

"Real Life *CSI*: This Is Not Your Average After-School Job: An Indiana Teen Spends Her Spare Time Working as a Certified Death Investigator," *Science World*, October 8, 2007.

Henry Fountain

"Plugging Holes in the Science of Forensics," *New York Times*, May 11, 2009.

Anand Giridharadas	"India's Novel Use of Brain Scans in Courts Is Debated," *New York Times*, September 14, 2008.
Amy Lennard Goehner, et al.	"Ripple Effect: Where *CSI* Meets Real *Law and Order*," *Time*, November 1, 2004.
Alex Johnson	"Already Under Fire, Crime Labs Cut to the Bone," MSNBC.com, February 23, 2010.
Jeffrey Kluger et al.	"How Science Solves Crimes," *Time*, October 21, 2002.
Roger Koppl	"Breaking Up the Forensics Monopoly: Eight Ways to Fix a Broken System," *Reason*, November 2007.
Roger Koppl	"What's Wrong with *CSI*," *Forbes*, June 2, 2008.
Steven D. Levitt	"Are the F.B.I.'s Probabilities About DNA Matches Crazy?" *New York Times*, August 19, 2008.
Solomon Moore	"In a Lab, an Ever-Growing Database of DNA Profiles," *New York Times*, May 11, 2009.
Ellen Nakashima	"From DNA of Family, a Tool to Make Arrests," *Washington Post*, April 21, 2008.
Adi Narayan	"The fMRI Brain Scan: A Better Lie Detector?" *Time*, July 20, 2009.

Virginia Postrel "Beautiful Minds: On Television Shows Like *CSI* and *Numb3rs*, Scientists Are Still Weird—but a Geeky Glamour Has Replaced the Old Stereotypes," *Atlantic*, September 2007.

Janet Raloff "Benched Science: Increasingly, Judges Decide What Science—If Any—a Jury Hears," *Science News*, October 8, 2005.

Brad Reagan "*CSI* Myths: The Shaky Science Behind Forensics," *Popular Mechanics*, August 2009.

Kit R. Roane and "The *CSI* Effect," *U.S. News & World* Dan Morrison *Report*, April 25, 2005.

Jeffrey Rosen "The Brain on the Stand," *New York Times*, March 11, 2007.

Michael J. Saks "The Coming Paradigm Shift in and Jonathan J. Forensic Identification Science," Koehler *Science*, August 5, 2005.

Fernanda Santos "Evidence from Bite Marks, It Turns Out, Is Not So Elementary," *New York Times*, January 28, 2007.

Jeffrey Toobin "The *CSI* Effect," *New Yorker*, May 2007.

USA Today "Real-life Police Forensics Don't Resemble 'CSI,'" February 19, 2009.

Index

A

"Abuse of discretion" standard, 32
Advanced Physics Lab (Johns Hopkins University), 173
Aerial photography, 153, 231
Alabama Computer Forensics Laboratories (ACFL), 76
Alabama District Attorneys Association, 76
Alito, Samuel A., Jr., 63
Altered states of mind, 161–162
American Association for the Advancement of Science, 84
American Board of Forensic Odontology, 224
American Justice (TV show), 122
Anderson, Bruce, 216
Annual Review of Law and Social Science (Saks, Faigman), 79–80
Anthropological Research Facility, 232
Anti-prosecution sentiment, 137–138
Armed Forces Institute of Pathology, 221
Asplen, Chris, 17
Assistant district attorney (ADA) survey results, 139
Autopsies, 31, 47, 48, 89, 232
   See also Multidetector computed tomography

B

Backlogged cases, 17–18, 86, 108, 109, 117, 130, 212

Balko, Radley, 44–49
Ballistic analysis. *See* Firearm analysis
Barak, Gregg, 124
Barsley, Robert, 226
Beddow, Michael, 208, 209
Bias
   autonomous labs and, 68
   cognitive, 74
   of experts, 45–47, 86, 139
   in latent print verifications, 81
   lie detection and, 188
   in media, 142
   pro-prosecution, 148
   researching, 30–31, 37
   subconscious, 48
Bite mark analysis, 29, 37, 38, 45, 224–226
Black Morris, 91
Blackmond, Brianna, 44
Blake, Robert, 99–100, 134–135
Blood oxygenation level dependent (BOLD) signals, 183–184
Blood pattern analysis
   advancements in, 199, 206–207
   CSI effect and, 95, 203–206, 232
   legislation of, 61
   overview, 202–203
Body fluid analysis, 45, 202
Bones (TV show), 106, 123
Bowers, Mike, 224, 226
Brain Fingerprinting
   altered states and, 161–162
   applications for, 156–157
   crime details and, 159–161

lie detection and, 158–159
media promotion of, 182–183
overview, 152–153
response to, 155–156
spread of, 162–163
Brain scanning
accuracy of, 164–166, 171
ethics of, 189–190
overview, 164
polygraph tests *vs.*, 182–183,
189–190
results of, 168–169
testing concerns, 187–190
wrongful accusations and, 167
See also Functional Magnetic
Resonance Imaging
Brecht, Bertolt, 69–70
Brewer, Kennedy, 44, 49–50, 225
Breyer, Samuel G., 63
Brilliant, Murray, 214, 216
Brooks, Levon, 44, 49–50, 225
Bundy, Ted, 224
Burden of proof, 113, 118, 119,
126, 133–134, 148
Burton, Robert, 153

C

California Criminalistics Institute,
209
California Law Review, 46
Caruso, David, 95
Cephos Corp., 164, 187, 189
Champod, Christophe, 81
Chase, Laura, 213
Chicago Tribune (newspaper), 30–
31, 45
Circumstantial evidence, 125, 128
Clairmont, Susan, 147
Clapper, James R., Jr., 173
Clinical ecology, 53

CODIS (Combined DNA Index
System) Database, 205–206
Cognitive bias. *See* Bias
Cold Case (TV show), 106, 123
Cole, Simon A., 50–60, 134, 141–
149
Computer Voice Stress Analyzer®
(CVSA®), 191, 194, 195, 196
Confrontation Right, 63
Contaminated evidence, 18, 31,
222
Convictions. *See* Criminal
conviction/trials; Wrongful
accusations/convictions
Counterintelligence Field Activity
agency, 173
Court TV (TV show), 122
Crime-fiction television. *See* CSI
effect; specific TV shows
Crime Gun Identification Act,
208–209
Crime Lab Report, 79–87
Crime labs
backlogs in, 17–18, 86, 108,
109, 117, 130, 212
certification of, 21
CSI effect and, 108–109
expert bias and, 45
result accuracy, 22, 62
underfunding of, 17–18, 117
Crime novels, 120
Criminal conviction/trials
CSI effect and, 106–109, 113–
121
defendants and, 114, 121
DNA testing and, 16–17
evidence and, 29, 31–32, 45
CSI: Crime Scene Investigation (TV
show). *See* CSI effect

CSI effect
blood pattern analysis and,
95, 203–206, 232
crime labs and, 108–109
criminal convictions and,
106–109, 113–121
CSI Infection as, 113–121
cultural values and, 147–149
DNA testing and, 93–94, 107
evidence and, 118–121, 134–
135, 147
eyewitness testimony and, 90,
96, 100, 106–107, 112, 125,
128, 146
forensic technology and, 16,
72, 102–103, 138–139
on judges, 106–112, 114
law enforcement and, 89, 106,
112, 116, 119, 132–140
overview, 89–90, 113–115,
132–134
perceptions of, 135–136
realism and, 92–97
show popularity and, 94–95,
127
validity of, 123–124, 132–134
victim's effect and, 145
CSI effect, media coverage
extent of, 143–145
overview, 141–143
review of, 145–147
social ramifications of, 147–
149
CSI effect, on attorneys
advantage of, 109–111, 138–
140
anti-prosecution sentiment
and, 137–138
defense lawyers and, 103–105,
117–118
district attorneys, 45–46

juror's expectations and, 96–
97, 99–101
verdicts and, 90, 106–107
CSI effect, on juries
acquittals and, 98–99, 106–
107, 114, 123
advantage of, 111–112
behavior and, 19, 89–90, 96,
115
crime labs and, 107–108
disadvantage of, 115–117
DNA evidence and, 96, 100,
128
evidence and, 99–101, 114,
126, 127–130, 138, 145
expert's credibility and, 146
influence of, 101–103, 124–
126
media coverage and, 143–147
overview, 91–92, 141–142
prosecutors and, 96–97
reasonable doubt and, 130–
131
unrealistic ideas of, 92–94

D

Dahmer, Jeffrey, 224
Damphouse, Kelly R., 191–197
Dateline NBC (TV show), 122
*Daubert v. Merrell Dow Pharma-
ceuticals, Inc.*, 31–33, 54
Dawson, Lorna, 228, 229–230
Decomposing bodies, 230–234
Dedman, Bill, 172–181
Defense Academy for Credibility
Assessment, 172, 175
Defense attorneys. *See* CSI effect,
on attorneys
Denniston, Lyle, 61–63

Department of Defense, 169, 172, 174–175, 181
Department of Homeland Security, 76
Derksen, Linda, 145, 148
DesPortes, Betty Layne, 96, 103
Devine, Elizabeth, 97
DeWolfe, Paul, 212
Digital forensic examiners, 76–77
Digital radiography (DR), 221
Dioso-Villa, Rachel, 134, 141–149
District attorneys, 45–46
DNA tests/evidence
  accuracy of, 22, 30, 82, 213
  advances in, 24–25, 33–34, 199, 212
  CODIS Database and, 205–206
  convictions with, 16–17
  CSI effect on, 93–94, 96, 100, 107, 128
  expectations of, 123–124, 134
  in homicide cases, 96–97, 100, 126
  NAS review of, 37–38, 65
  for non-violent crimes, 211–214
  physical appearance and, 214–216
  in rape cases, 96–97, 126, 128
  soil analysis and, 229
  underuse of, 16–18
  validity of, 37–38
  wrongful convictions and, 36, 44
Driscoll, Kate, 232–233
Drowning deaths, 219–221
Drug analysis/toxicology report
  accuracy of, 30–31
  challenging, 61
  prosecuting attorneys and, 74
  voice stress analysis and, 192, 194–196
Drug deals/smuggling, 77, 222–223
Duncan, Gary, 96–97
Durst, Robert, 91

E

Edwards, Harry, 68
Electroencephalographic (EEG), 152, 182, 187
Ethical Rules of Professional Conduct, 117
Evidence collection
  absence of, 137
  admission of, 30–32
  challenging, 62–63
  circumstantial, 125, 128
  contaminated, 18, 31, 222
  convictions with, 29, 31–32, 45
  court admission and, 31–32, 83–84
  explanatory, 117–118
  jury demand for, 99–101, 125–126, 138
  lack of standards in, 41–43
  masking, 48–49
  meaning of, 118–121
  negative evidence witnesses, 93–94
  of non-DNA, 39–40
  preservation of, 31
  probative value of, 136
  research of, 80–81
  trace evidence, 37, 39, 185, 227–228, 230
  validity of, 40–41, 138–139
  verdicts from, 127–128
  witness testimony *vs.*, 100, 135

See also CSI effect; DNA tests/
evidence; Expert evidence/
testimony; Fingerprint
evidence/analysis
Expert evidence/testimony
admission of, 30–34
bias in, 45–47, 81
in bite mark analysis, 225
on Brain Fingerprinting, 162
code of ethics and, 67
credibility of, 25, 38, 42, 146
cross-examination and, 17, 61
CSI effect and, 96, 107, 146
in DNA testing, 28
forensic science and, 18, 21
interpretation in, 29
in pattern identification, 86,
202
poor training and, 69
proof of reliability in, 52, 54,
56
Explanatory evidence, 117–118
Eye color characteristics, 215–216
Eyewitness testimony
CSI effect and, 90, 100, 106–
107, 112, 125, 128
errors in, 119
forensic testing and, 110
physical evidence and, 135

F

Faigman, David, 79, 81, 85–87
Farwell, Lawrence, 154–162
Federal Bureau of Investigation
(FBI), 22, 41, 51, 59, 144, 156–
157, 233–234
Federal Rules of Evidence, 31–32,
116
Fiber analysis, 45, 67, 68, 107
Fienberg, Stephen, 172, 176, 179–
181

Filbert, Margarethe, 227
Fingerprint evidence/analysis
accuracy of, 30–31, 45, 50–52,
57–59
challenging, 61
cognitive bias and, 74
error rates and, 18, 29, 48, 51,
53, 56
examiner's fallacy in, 54–56
as junk science, 52–54
jury demand for, 125, 126,
129
print comparisons, 37
scientific abuse and, 59–60
state-of-the-art quality of, 95
Firearm analysis
bullet matching, 206
CSI effect and, 125
DNA tests *vs.*, 82
flaws with, 209–210
microstamping, 208–210
validity of, 37, 84
Fisher, Barry, 94
Fitzpatrick, William, 200
Fluoroscopy, 217, 218
fMRI. *See* Functional Magnetic
Resonance Imaging
Food and Drug Administration
(FDA), 39
Forensic Files (TV show), 91
Forensic Magazine, 17
Forensic practitioners/analysts, 28,
61–63, 69, 76–77
Forensic Science Graduate Group,
209
Forensic Science Initiative, 98
Forensic science/technology
abuse of, 59–60
accuracy of, 21, 30, 33, 69
advances in, 25
changes to, 67–69

on decomposing bodies, 230–234
disciplines in, 27–29, 84–85
disparities in, 26–27
economic justification for, 83–84
evidence of research, 80–81
expert testimony and, 18, 21
objectivity of, 138
social changes and, 82–85
standardization of, 27
technology revolution and, 129–130
truth of, 32–34, 45–46
types of, 199–200
validity of, 21–22, 38–40, 66–67, 133, 185
value of, 16–19
wording of, 86–87
See also CSI effect; DNA tests/evidence; Evidence collection; Firearm analysis; Juries/jury influence; National Academy of Sciences; Wrongful accusations/convictions; specific analyses
Forensic science/technology, fraud/errors
CSI effect and, 96
expert's bias, 45–47
overview, 44–45
reforms needed for, 47–49
rivalrous redundancy, 47–48
weeding out, 62
Forensic science/technology, standardization
"abuse of discretion," 32
for digital forensic examiners, 76–77
in fingerprint evidence, 50
Frye Standard, 103

lack of, 27, 41–43
quality of, 87
48 Hours Mystery (TV show), 122
Fourth Amendment rights, 200
Frye Standard, 103
Functional Magnetic Resonance Imaging (fMRI)
accuracy of, 187–188
assumptions about, 183–184
as convincing, 185–186
for lie detection, 152, 153, 165–170
media promotion of, 182–183
results of, 184

G

Galileo's Revenge (Huber), 52–53
Galton, Francis, 84
Gang firearms, 209–210
Gas chromatography, 206
Gene-sequencing, 212
Genetic markers, 22
Geoforensics. *See* Soil analysis
Geoforensics and Information Management for crime Investigation (GIMI), 230
George, Mark, 166, 167, 168, 171
Goddard, Calvin, 84
Grabherr, Silke, 222–223
Grand juries, 98–99, 103
Graybow, Martha, 133
Greely, Hank, 166, 170, 188, 189–190
Grinder, JB, 161
Gun analysis. *See* Firearm analysis
Gunshot residue, 99, 100
Gunshot wounds, 220–221

H

Hair color characteristics, 215–216
Hair microscopy, 30, 37
Hand-held lie detector
    accuracy of, 175–176, 179–181
    decision-making and, 177
    overview, 172–174
    polygraph test *vs.*, 174–175
    as triage device, 176–178
    validity studies for, 178–179
Handwriting analysis, 100
Harcke, H. Theodore, 221
Harrington v. State of Iowa, 162
Harvey, Elizabeth, 145, 148
Hayne, Steven, 44
Hedge, Phyllis, 200
Heinrick, Jeffrey, 98–105
Helton, Julie, 161
Henderson, Carol, 65–66, 69
Hirschhorn, Robert, 91, 92
Homicide cases, 17, 31, 37, 96–97,
    100, 126
Houck, Max, 65–67, 68–69, 98
House (TV show), 187
*How William Shatner Changed the
    World* (TV show), 101
Howitt, David, 210
Huber, Peter, 52–53
Huizenga, Joel T., 165
Hulsey, Brannon, 232, 233
Human intelligence interrogators
    (HUMINT), 178–179
Hyperlexis (too much law), 149

I

ID Dynamics, 208
Illes, Judy, 170

Imaging technology. *See* Functional Magnetic Resonance Imaging; Multidetector computed tomography
Innocence Project (advocacy group), 18, 35–36, 44, 46, 119, 225
Innocent people. *See* Wrongful accusations/convictions
The Internet, 51, 116, 122, 129
Interpretation of evidence, 29

J

Jackson, Michael, 99
Johnson, L. Thomas, 45, 224, 226
Junk science, 52–54, 224
Juries/jury influence
    cognitive bias and, 46
    grand juries and, 98–99, 103
    judicial truth, 32–34
    non-DNA evidence and, 39
    petite juries, 98–99
    polygraph tests *vs.*, 170, 189
    TV watching by, 124–126
    voir dire and, 110, 111
    See also CSI effect, on juries
Justice, Connie, 204–205

K

Kennedy, Anthony M., 63
Kim, Young, 124
Kluger, Jeffrey, 89–90
Koppl, Roger, 44–49
Krane, Dan, 96
Krapohl, Donald, 172, 175, 176–177, 181
Krone, Ray, 225

L

Lafayette Instrument Co., 173
Laken, Steven, 164, 169, 189
Landscape reconstruction, 230
Langleben, Daniel, 188
Latent print identification. *See*
  Fingerprint evidence/analysis
Law & Order (TV show), 91, 94–
  95, 106, 116, 122, 127
Law enforcement
  backlogs and, 18
  bias and, 74
  Brain Fingerprinting and, 162
  cognitive rationalization by,
    139–140
  CSI effect and, 89, 106, 112,
    116, 119, 132–140
  decomposing bodies and,
    233–234
  DNA testing and, 24, 226
  forensic science and, 23–26,
    38, 68–69, 145, 166
  funding, 26–27, 40, 66, 130
  lie detection and, 174, 191,
    192, 197
  protection by, 33, 52, 77–78
  training of, 76, 216
  wrongful convictions and, 35,
    37
  See also Crime labs; Forensic
    science/technology
Lawson, Tamara F., 113–121
Layered Voice Analysis™ (LVA),
  191, 194, 195, 196
Lefebvre, Nathan, 207
Levy, Angela D., 220
Lie detection. *See* Brain fingerprinting; Brain scanning; Functional Magnetic Resonance Imaging; Hand-held lie detector;
  Polygraph tests

Littlefield, Melissa, 182–186
Lizotte, Todd, 208
Llewellyn, Barbara, 97
Locard, Edmond, 227

M

MacDonell, Leon, 206
Manning, Peter, 143
Maricopa County Attorney's Of-
  fice (MCAO), 101, 109, 111, 144
Marquis, Joshua K., 96, 106–112
Martin, Matt, 202–207
Masking evidence, 48–49
Matlock (TV show), 116
Matson, Barry, 71–78
Matthews, J. Howard, 84
MDCT technology. *See* Multide-
  tector computed tomography
Meaning of evidence, 118–121
Medical examiner system, 25
Mehta, Aalok, 187–190
Melendez-Diaz v. Massachusetts, 61
Melton, Terry, 97
Mercer, Stephen, 211, 213
Microscopic hair analysis. *See* Hair
  microscopy
*Midwest Forensic Resource Center
  (MFRC)*, 81
Midwest Forensic Resources Cen-
  ter (Iowa State), 225
Miller, David, 230
Miller, Mark, 206
Mitchell, Melissa, 182–186
Mitotyping Technologies, 97
Moore, Patricia, 48
Morse, Dan, 211–214
Multidetector computed tomogra-
  phy (MDCT) scanners
    in drowning deaths, 219–221

drug smuggling and, 222–223
speed of, 218–219
uses for, 217–218
Murder cases. *See* Homicide cases
Murphy, Wendy, 103–104
Murray, Louise, 227–231

N

National Academy of Sciences
(NAS)
compliance with, 76–78
DNA testing and, 37–38, 65
fingerprint evidence and, 51
forensic technology and, 21,
35–36
hand-held lie detectors and,
172, 175, 179
negative impact of, 74–76
overview, 71–72
polygraph tests and, 174
post-conviction exoneration
and, 40
prosecuting attorneys and,
72–74
solutions from, 64–66
National Computer Forensics Institute (NCFI), 76–77
National District Attorneys Association, 93, 103–104
National Forensic Academy, 233–
234
*National Forensic DNA Study Re-
port*, 17
National Geographic (magazine),
143
National Institute of Forensic Science, 68
National Institute of Justice (NIJ),
17–18, 41, 191, 194

National Research Council, 21,
24–34, 210
NCIS (TV show), 106
Negative evidence witnesses,
93–94
Neufeld, Peter, 35–43, 225
New York Times (newspaper), 22
9/11. *See* September 11, 2001 at-
tacks
No Lie MRI Inc., 165, 187
Nuclear DNA analysis. *See* DNA
tests/evidence
Numbers (TV show), 123

O

O'Brien, Angela, 44
Odontology. *See* Bite mark analy-
sis
Oklahoma City Arrestee Drug
Abuse Monitoring (ADAM)
study, 196
Oklahoma Department of Mental
Health and Substance Abuse Ser-
vices, 192
Osborne, Mike, 232–234

P

P300 MERMER (Memory and
Encoding Related Multi-facet
Electronic Response), 154–155
Page, Douglas, 217–223
Paint analysis, 45
Pattern identification disciplines,
84–85
Pellegrino, Evan, 214–216
People v. Hill, 72
The People's Court (TV show), 102

Perry Mason (TV show), 101–102, 116

Petite jury, 98–99

Plant debris analysis, 229

Podlas, Kimberlianne, 132–140, 146

Polygraph tests
accuracy of, 151–152, 172
assumptions about, 183–184
brain-based tests *vs.*, 182–183, 189–190
Defense Department use of, 174
hand-held lie detectors *vs.*, 174–175
juries *vs.*, 170, 189
limitations of, 193
physical reactions with, 182–183

Popp, Georg, 227

Preliminary Credibility Assessment Screening System (PCASS). *See* Hand-held lie detector

Probative value of evidence, 136

Proof of reliability, 52, 54, 56

Prosecuting attorneys, 72–74
See also CSI effect, on attorneys

R

Radar interferometry, 231

Ramirez, Richard, 100

Ramsey, JonBenét, 205

Rape cases, 17, 37, 96–97, 126, 128, 158

Reasonable doubt, 130, 134–135, 144

Reflected Ultra-Violet Imaging System (RUVIS), 207

Richardson, Drew, 156–157, 162

Richmond, Todd, 224–226

Risinger, Michael, 46

Ritter, Malcolm, 164–171

Rivalrous redundancy, 47–48

Roberts, John G., Jr., 63

Rosen, Jeffrey, 200

Royce, Dan, 207

Ruffell, Alastair, 231

Rutty, Guy N., 218–219

S

Saks, Michael J., 79, 81, 85–87

Saliva testing, 45, 211, 215

Salon (magazine), 153

Satellite photography, 231

Scalia, Antonin, 61, 62–63

Schwarzenegger, Arnold, 208

Schweitzer & Saks study, 120

Science (magazine), 51

Science, Technology & Human Values (journal), 182

Scientific American (magazine), 143

Scientific Working Group (SWG), 27

September 11, 2001 attacks, 182, 186

Sexual assault cases. *See* Rape cases

Shaibani, Saami, 44, 46

Shaken baby syndrome, 48

Shapiro, Robert, 164, 166

Shelton, Donald E., 120, 122–131, 146

Simon, Sam, 154–163

Simpson, O.J., 112, 164

Sixth Amendment rights, 114

60 Minutes (news show), 55

Skin analysis
   bite marks and, 29, 37, 38, 45, 224–226
   DNA tests and, 205, 214
   pigmentation characteristics, 214–215
Social changes in forensic science, 82–85
Soil analysis (geoforensics), 227–231
SoilFit initiative, 228
Spence, Sean, 169
Stanford Center for Law and the Biosciences, 166
Star Trek (TV show), 101
State v. Columbus, 56
Statute of limitations, 36
Supreme Court (U.S.), 17, 31–32, 54, 61, 83–84, 151, 170
Sutton, T. Paulette, 202–205
Sweet, David, 226

T

Testimony. See Expert evidence/testimony; Eyewitness testimony
Thomas, Clarence, 63
Thompson, David, 178–179
Thompson, Robert, 95
Time (magazine), 89, 143
Time Team (TV show), 230
Tool mark analysis, 37, 38, 82
Trace evidence, 37, 39, 185, 227–228, 230
Tracing Truth: A Cultural History of Deception Detection (Littlefield), 185
Tulleners, Fred, 209–210

U

United States v. Crisp, 56
United States v. Havvard, 56
United States v. Mitchell, 56
United States v. Scheffer, 151
U.S. News & World Report (magazine), 143
U.S. Supreme Court, 17, 31–32, 54, 61, 83–84, 151, 170
USA Today (newspaper), 102

V

Valenzuela, Robert, 216
Vendemia, Jennifer, 169
Voice stress analysis
   accuracy of, 191–193, 195
   controversy over, 197
   detection results from, 193
   drug analysis with, 192, 194–196
   as lying deterrent, 195–196
   research studies on, 194
Voir dire (jury selection process), 110, 111

W

Waller, James, 177
Walsh, Paul, 93
Wang, Wendy, 208–210
Warren, Earl, 83–84
Washington Post (newspaper), 200
West, Michael, 44, 46, 225
Wethal, Tabatha, 64–70
Wickenheiser, Ray, 211, 212, 213
Willing, Richard, 91–97
Wilson, Dominic J., 211
Wilson, Rebecca, 233–234
Without a Trace (TV show), 123

Wrongful accusations/convictions
    bias in, 48–49
    brain scanning and, 167
    from forensic technology, 21–
      23, 33
    law enforcement and, 35, 37
    overturning, 44
    post-conviction exoneration,
      40

X

X-rays, 217, 218

Y

Yale Law Journal, 104
Young, Myron, 173

Z

Zuicker, Anthony E., 102